The Last Commando

Brian H. Jones

The Last Commando
The story of the Transvaal Boers –
expansion, curtailment, demise and myth

*The Last Commando: The story of the Transvaal Boers
– expansion, curtailment, demise and myth*
ISBN 978 1 76041 711 6
Copyright © Brian H. Jones 2019
Cover: Kirsten Harlech-Jones
Map: Elwyn Harlech-Jones

First published 2019 by
GINNINDERRA PRESS
PO Box 3461 Port Adelaide 5015
www.ginninderrapress.com.au

Contents

1	In the Beginning	7
2	Getting On With It	15
3	Christians and Heathens	20
4	A Rebellious People	29
5	Identity and Expansion	35
6	Appropriation and Extermination	42
7	The Gonaquas and Stuurman	49
8	Colonial Borders	56
9	The Eastern Frontier	70
10	Commandos and 'Bastards'	77
11	Dissatisfaction	85
12	The Great Trek	94
13	The Transvaal	104
14	Keeping Order	117
15	Relationships	127
16	Size and Isolation	133
17	Annexation and After	143
18	Gold	153
19	The *Uitlanders*	163
20	The Jameson Raid and War	173
21	Civil Religion, Afrikanerdom and the Republic	187
Notes		196
Works Cited		198

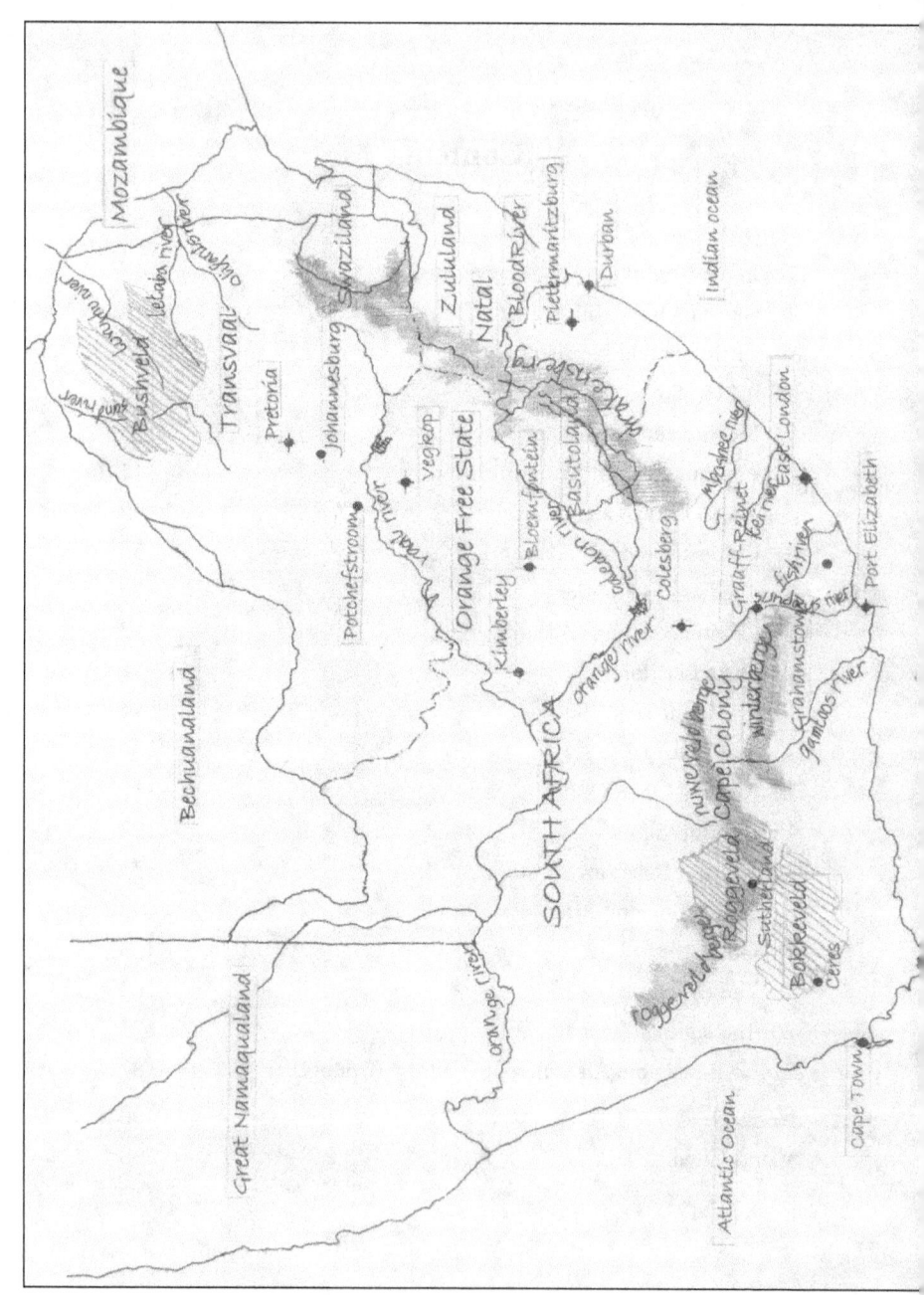

1

In the Beginning

I live in a country town in New South Wales, Australia. As in most Australian towns and cities, there is a memorial to the local men who fought in the Boer War. This memorial, which stands in the park in the centre of the town, was unveiled on 14 November 1904 and records the names of eighty-two men who served in the war. Twenty-four of those were officers, NCOs and special ranks, which included one farrier sergeant, one shoeing smith and two trumpeters. The inscription shows

Goulburn, NSW, war memorial plaque.

that four troopers died in South Africa. Three of those passed away in Pretoria, which probably means that they died in hospital of wounds or dysentery. One trooper was killed on 10 May 1901 at Korannafontein in the western Transvaal, where the recently arrived 2nd NSW Mounted Regiment, of which he was a member, came off badly in an encounter with a Boer force that was led by the charismatic commanders Koos de la Rey and Jan Smuts. This unfortunate recruit had only been in South Africa for three weeks when a Boer bullet ended his life.

The Boer War took place when the British Empire was at is zenith. In 1899, at the start of the war, Queen Victoria had been on the throne for sixty-two years, while the Empire was said to encompass about one-quarter of the world's population. When war broke out during October 1899, such was the enthusiasm for Queen and country that men from all over the Empire rushed to volunteer, cheered on by enthusiastic crowds. Because this was a white man's war, the volunteers mainly came from the United Kingdom and the Dominions (as they were called later), which included Australians, Canadians and New Zealanders, and South Africans who identified with the British cause. However, although people with darker skins did not carry weapons, or so both sides averred, black South Africans provided support to fighters on both sides of the conflict, while thousands of Indians, including Mahatma Gandhi (who was then living in South Africa), served as British auxiliaries.

Few among the cheering crowds who supported the war at its key moments would have been thinking about the following lines from Kipling's poem 'Recessional', which he wrote to mark Victoria's jubilee in 1897; even fewer would have identified with the sentiment expressed there:

> Far-called our navies melt away;
>   On dune and headland sinks the fire:
> Lo, all our pomp of yesterday
>   Is one with Nineveh and Tyre!
> Judge of the Nations, spare us yet,
> Lest we forget – lest we forget!

It did not take long for the melting away to begin. Less than twenty years later, amid the shocks and slaughter of the First World War, the Empire commenced the path of decline that would reduce the pomp of yesterday to nothing but a distant memory by the end of the century.

This book is not about the Anglo-Boer War. Instead, it looks at the origins, nature, world views and organisation of the Boers and their society. It says little about the war, except as an event that brought about the demise of the two independent Boer states, namely the Transvaal (the South African Republic) and the Orange Free State. When the Boer generals surrendered on 31 May 1902, the story of the Boers as independent entities came to an end. Although something new did arise from defeat, humiliation and suffering, it is not the concern of this book. That something new was Afrikanerdom, Afrikaner nationalism and apartheid, all of which have been discussed, analysed and chronicled by many writers.

Although I go over a lot of ground that has been covered elsewhere, I have put this book together in my own way and from my own perspective. When I say that the ground has been covered elsewhere, I do not mean that I have knowingly copied material. Although the many books that have been written about the Boers will have influenced my thoughts, I have deliberately avoided almost all secondary sources while I have been writing this book. Instead, I have tried to look at the subject with an open and fresh mind. Mainly, I consulted primary sources, most of them written during the nineteenth century, that have the advantage of being much closer to the time and subject about which I am writing. In addition, I have added my own knowledge and experience to the mix.

Having said that, let's get down to it...

Arthur Conan Doyle is famous for being the creator of Sherlock Holmes. Doyle was also a highly qualified medical practitioner who volunteered to serve as a doctor in South Africa during the war. He was there for three months, between March and June 1900, and only a few months later he published a history of the war. At the time, along with most supporters of the British cause, Doyle believed that the war was almost over when his book was published in September 1900. The British had occupied both Boer capital cities, the Boer forces had scattered, and many of the Boer fighters had either surrendered, had been captured or had given up the struggle. To Doyle, as to most observers, it was obvious that Boer resistance had collapsed and that the end of the war was at hand. In addition, to put the seal on these reverses, Paul Kruger, the president of the South African Republic, the icon of Boer resistance and the craggy, iron-willed embodiment of the spirit of his people, had gone into exile in Europe.

Doyle wrote this about Kruger's departure:

> On September 11th [1900] an incident had occurred which must have shown the most credulous believer in Boer prowess that their cause was indeed lost. On that date Paul Kruger, a refugee from the country which he had ruined, arrived at Lourenço Marques, abandoning his beaten commandos and his deluded burghers. How much had happened since those distant days when as a little herdsboy he had walked behind the bullocks on the great northward trek. How piteous this ending to all his strivings and his plottings! A life which might have closed amid the reverence of a nation and the admiration of the world was destined to finish in exile, impotent and undignified.

The old president died in Switzerland during 1904, so Doyle was correct when he described exile as an end to all of Kruger's strivings. However, like almost everyone except a small number of Boers, Doyle was wrong about the end of the war. It continued for a further eighteen months; and they were harrowing months, with guerrilla fighting, a scorched earth policy and escalating deaths of women and children in concentration camps. In fact, even to this day, many Afrikaners have not forgotten what happened in those dreadful, squalid camps where one-quarter of all Boer women and children, about 26,000 in all, died of disease and starvation.

However, even though the war continued for much longer than

anticipated, it was inevitable that the might of the Empire would prevail. The end came on 31 May 1902 when the exhausted *bittereindes* (bitter-enders or hardliners), the ragged remnants of the Boer forces, capitulated by signing a peace treaty. One of the main reasons for making peace, which was almost unconditional, was that most of the Boer representatives believed that a prolongation of hostilities would entail so many more deaths of women and children in the camps that the future of the *volk* (the nation) would be endangered.

For the record, Doyle updated his book sixteen times before the final edition was published during September 1902. By that time, Doyle, who was an inveterate imperialist like most members of his race and class, acknowledged that the Boers were

> the most formidable antagonist who ever crossed the path of Imperial Britain… Napoleon and all his veterans have never treated us so roughly as these hard-bitten farmers with their ancient theology and their inconveniently modern rifles.

Doyle was only one among many British commentators who paid similar, grudging tributes to the determination and resilience of the Boers. However, as I said earlier, this book is not about the war. The narrative begins a long time earlier and ends with the war, followed by a short coda.

At this point, I am going to return to Paul Kruger because he was the quintessential Boer. In fact, his life more than spanned the period of existence of the Boer political entity that was known as the Transvaal, or the South African Republic (*Zuid-Afrikaansche Republiek*). As a young man, Kruger was a member of one of the vanguard groups of trekkers who settled in the territory and founded the state that became the Transvaal or ZAR. Then, more than sixty years later, he left it as the country's last president, at the time when the ZAR ceased to exist. In fact, Kruger was so quintessentially a Transvaal Boer, and he so dominated its history and politics, that even today he seems to bestride it like the fabled Colossus.

Kruger was a larger-than-life figure who was loved and respected, even revered, by his friends and admirers, and was reviled and mocked by his many enemies and detractors. For an insight into Kruger's idiosyncrasies, we have this report by Joshua Slocum, an American, who was the first man to sail around the world single-handed. He wrote this about his meeting with Kruger in Pretoria in 1898:

> His Excellency [Kruger] received me cordially enough; but my friend Judge Beyers, the gentleman who presented me, by mentioning that I was on a voyage around the world, unwittingly gave great offense to the venerable statesman, which we both regretted deeply. Mr. Krüger corrected the judge rather sharply, reminding him that the world is flat. 'You don't mean round the world,' said the president; 'it is impossible! You mean in the world. Impossible!' he said, 'impossible!' and not another word did he utter either to the judge or to me. The judge looked at me and I looked at the judge, who should have known his ground, so to speak, and Mr. Krüger glowered at us both. My friend the judge seemed embarrassed, but I was delighted; the incident pleased me more than anything else that could have happened. It was a nugget of information quarried out of Oom Paul, some of whose sayings are famous. Of the English he said, 'They took first my coat and then my trousers.' He also said, 'Dynamite is the corner-stone of the South African Republic.' Only unthinking people call President Krüger dull.

One of Kruger's well-known practices as president was to sit on his *stoep* (veranda) in Pretoria every morning, drinking coffee and smoking his big meerschaum pipe. There, he was available for an audience with anyone who wished to speak with him. Even this apparently innocuous practice provoked controversy. For instance, a foreign detractor called Kruger's house 'the throne of a copper-riveted autocracy' and accused Kruger of being a despotic, psalm-singing old Boer who loved to sit on his *stoep* from five o'clock in the morning, drinking the first of many cups of strong coffee.

Incidentally, I had it on good authority from my grandfather that, as a schoolboy on his way to the English school (my grandfather was an *uitlander* – see later) in Pretoria during the 1890s, every morning he would pass the old president, sitting on his *stoep*. My grandfather told me that he would raise his cap and greet President Kruger with the words, '*Dag, Oom* Paul (Good morning, Uncle Paul).' Even a schoolboy could greet the president...

Another story is that during one of Kruger's visits to England on state business, a young English nobleman proudly told Kruger that his father had been the Viceroy of India. In reply, Kruger dryly told the young man that his father had been a shepherd. Moreover, according to at least one account, during a diplomatic mission to Britain, Kruger and his fellow emissary did not have enough money to pay their hotel bills and had to be helped by sympathisers.

Although these incidents go some way to illustrate Kruger's simplicity and modest style of life both as a citizen and a head of state, they do not explain it. On the contrary: there have been many heads of state who, despite very humble beginnings, have enjoyed great wealth and ceremony when in power. Lowly birth has never prevented most powerful personages from enriching themselves, enjoying opulence, surrounding themselves with security, pomp and elaborate protocol, and putting up barriers between themselves and the common people.

An Australian connection – plaque at the entrance to the (Boer-built) Old Fort, Johannesburg.

This being the case, it seems that Kruger's humble birth only partly explains the simplicity of his lifestyle. As we will see, it was a product of the Boers' world view: it reflected a way of looking at their relationships with each other, their relationships with the peoples with whom they interacted, their understanding of the world and the universe, and their relationship with the God whose Word provided them with assurances, comfort and guidance.

Kruger's friends and admirers extolled his virtues, which included personal bravery and courage, hardihood, perseverance, simplicity (but not naivety), a strong, fundamentalist faith and unswerving devotion to the cause of the *volk*. In contrast, Kruger's enemies and detractors portrayed him as bigoted, narrow-minded, autocratic, isolationist, uncultured, inflexible and backwoods in outlook and beliefs.

To both their friends and their enemies, the Boers were Kruger writ large.

2

Getting On With It

I will weave parts of this account around the life of Paul Kruger, because so much of his life and experiences mirrored, and even shaped, the history of the Boers. Writing in 1901, James Cappon expressed the close connection like this:

> Paul Kruger is a living link between the Boers of to-day and the wild Jan Bothas and Bezuidenhouts of the past. He is a Boer of the Great Trek, a genuine son of the savage soil of Bruintjes Hoogte,[1] with the fierce memories of the old Graaff-Reinet frontier still living in his heart, fresher probably than the things of yesterday.

When Cappon's book was published, the Boers of today to whom he referred were the men who then were fighting against the British in the (Second) Anglo-Boer War. Perhaps Cappon's assessment was overly dramatic, even melodramatic; nevertheless, it contained an essential truth when he said that Kruger was a living link between the Boers who fought the war and the time before there was even a Transvaal republic – namely, the time when thousands of Boers, most of them from the eastern frontier of the Cape Colony, joined the Great Trek and, with their wagons, oxen and herds, moved into the uncharted interior of Southern Africa.

Kruger began his memoirs by saying that he was born on 10 October 1825. At the age of nine, together with his parents and his uncles, they left Vaalbank Farm in the Colesberg district of the Cape Colony. Although there is doubt about the matter, it seems that Kruger was born in the Cradock district, before the family moved to the

Paul Kruger memorial in Church Square, Pretoria.

Colesberg district. He described his parents as simple farmers and said that he grew up on the farm like other farmers' lads, 'looking after the herds and lending a hand in the fields'.

In the Cape Colony, before they trekked northwards, the Krugers were frontier people. In fact, although Paul Kruger refers to having grown up in the Colesberg district, the town of Colesberg was only founded in 1830. When the family left the area five years later, during 1835, it is likely that Colesberg consisted of only a few simple buildings. The nearest town of any consequence was Graaff-Reinet, which lay about 200 kilometres southward. In those days, travelling in an ox wagon over rocky and unprepared terrain, following the tracks of other wagons, the trip would have taken at least ten days but probably much longer. (Backhouse records that an ox wagon at its usual rate of travelling would cover about three miles per hour, or just less than five kilometres per hour, but would only do two and a half miles per hour on longer journeys.) Considering that the total time spent on the trip could amount to nearly one month, with at least ten days outward bound, a number of days spent in town, and then at least ten days on the return journey, it is clear that an expedition such as this would be undertaken infrequently, and then only for very good reason. Nor was it possible just to drop in on the neighbours: in those days, the nearest neighbours could be many hours away by horseback, and a visit by ox wagon would take even longer.

The lives of Boers like the Kruger family, who were colonists on the eastern and north-eastern frontiers of the Colony, are relevant to this work because most of the Transvaal Boers originated from those districts; as Cappon says,

> There, on the lands lying along the Little and Great Fish Rivers, which formed a natural, though ill-kept and partly disputed boundary between the colony and the territory of the *Kosa-Kaffir* tribes, dwelt a race of rough frontier farmers possessing large grazing farms, on which, with the aid of slaves and Hottentot servants, they reared great herds of cattle and sheep... Amongst those names the most frequent are those of Prinsloos, Burghers, Krugers, Jouberts, Erasmuses, Bothas, Smits...

The writer estimated that ninety-eight per cent of the Boers who made the Great Trek, from 1836 to 1839, came from the district of Graaff-Reinet alone. During the 1830s, the Colesberg region, home of the young Paul Kruger, would have been within this extensive district. As I said, Cappon was writing during the Anglo-Boer War and many of the men who were fighting against the British were the direct descendants of the men who had trekked northwards from the frontier districts of the Cape Colony during the 1830s. The memories and experiences of the old frontier in the colony would still have been fresh among these sons and grandsons of the trekkers who had abandoned their farms and homes because of their opposition to the British.

Therefore, to understand the Transvaal Boers, I will look at the history, culture and beliefs of the frontier Boers at the time that they left the colony and headed northwards for parts (almost) unknown, in search of places where they could govern themselves, free of external constraint.

The frontier Boers were the descendants of the free burghers who had been allowed to remain in the Cape during the mid-seventeenth century when their contracts with the Dutch East India Company (the VOC) expired after the Dutch settlement at the Cape was founded in 1652.

What sorts of people were the free burghers? One writer said that most of the VOC's seamen and soldiers, some of whom became free burghers, were largely press-ganged into service; he disparagingly labelled the group as 'a motley crew of spendthrifts, vagabonds, and simpletons, the very refuse of Europe'. However, Henry Cloete wrote that although his ancestor, Jacob Cloten, one of the original seventeen free burghers, had an 'ambitious and rebellious temperament' he was also 'a man of family and education…' It is possible that not all of the first free burghers were vagrants and wastrels.

Whatever the natures of those early free burghers, their numbers were soon swelled and their characters were influenced by the arrival of other settlers who appear to have had steady and industrious habits. Fisher noted that during 1685 'fifty respectable Dutch families' were sent out and settled on farms in the Stellenbosch district. In addition, there were 'forty-eight superior selected orphans' who, it was hoped, would 'reform the morals of the free burghers'. This was followed soon afterwards in 1688 by the arrival of a group of Huguenots who, after fleeing to the Netherlands to escape religious oppression in their native France, were resettled at the Cape. There were ninety-seven Huguenot families, comprising about 300 men, women, and children. Fisher said of them, 'They carried with them, amongst other things, the twin blessings of wine and the Bible.' Many of the Huguenots were people of good education; some were manufacturers, and others were vine-growers and gardeners. One of their most enduring legacies is the Cape wine industry.

Even at the end of the nineteenth century, which was 250 years after the first free burghers settled at the Cape, the Boers still honoured their joint Dutch-Hugenot ancestry. For instance, in his call to arms at the beginning of the Anglo-Boer War, Francis William Reitz, state secretary of the ZAR, invoked a heritage of suffering, oppression and fortitude to inspire the burghers in their struggle. Depicting the war against the British Empire as another seminal moment in the history of the *volk*, Reitz wrote,

> Our forefathers did not pale before the terrors of the Spanish Inquisition, but entered upon the great struggle for Freedom and Right against even the mighty Philip, unmindful of the consequences. Nor could the rack and the persecuting bands of Louis XIV tame or subdue the spirit of our fathers. Neither Alva nor Richelieu were able to compass the triumph of tyranny over the innate sentiment of Freedom and Independence in our forefathers.

Philip and Alva refer to the King of Spain and his bloodthirsty military commander during the war of independence that the Dutch waged again Spain, while Richelieu refers to the prime mover in the oppression that drove the Huguenots from their native France to take refuge in the Netherlands.

3

Christians and Heathens

Fisher thought that the biggest contribution of the Huguenots to the character of the Boers was the addition of what he called 'an earnest religious feeling'. Religion was a dominant aspect of the Boers' culture and anyone who wrote about them was sure to mention it, sooner rather than later. As we have seen, Conan Doyle, for instance, referred to the Boers' 'ancient theology', while H.M. Stanley mockingly referred to a discussion in the first *raad* (council or parliament) of the South African Republic (Transvaal/ZAR), during which President Paul Kruger, in supporting his argument, said that Isaiah had been told by the Lord that Israel had been punished because the rulers had not listened to the voice of the poor. Next, said Stanley, another speaker stated that the Lord had enjoined that the rich, not the rulers, should help the poor, and Isaiah had not been told that the poor were to be helped with other people's money. Stanley continued by mocking Kruger's intellect as well as at the general quality of a parliamentary chamber that settled its debates by reference to an Old Testament prophet.

In his memoirs, Paul Kruger referred to the central place that religion played in the lives of Boers when he said that every Boer taught his children to read and write and, above all, instructed them in God's Word. Instruction took place around the dinner table, where the children had to read out passages from the Bible as well as repeat parts from memory. This, said Kruger, was how his father taught him about the Bible. Writing just before the end of the eighteenth century, Barrow reported that hardly any books were seen in Boer farmhouses in the interior of the Cape, apart from the Bible and a book of psalms.

Barrow continued by saying that a long grace was said before every meal, and that every day began with the singing of one of the psalms before sunrise. Furthermore, said Barrow, the Boers were scrupulous in attending church, even if 'the performance of this duty costs many of them a journey of several days'. They would make the journey to attend the quarterly *Nagmaal* (Communion), about which more later.

With religion so central to the life of the Boers, Kruger was only able to stand for election as president of the republic when the law was amended to allow members of his Dopper Church, which was Calvinist but not Dutch Reformed, to be eligible for office. Until then, said Kruger, according to the constitution of the ZAR, the *Hervormde* (Reformed) Church was the state church and whoever was not a member of the *Hervormde* Church was not a fully qualified burgher.

Even at the end of his life, with the Boers defeated and the independence of the republics at an end, Kruger retained his religious faith. He concluded his memoirs by saying that during the peace negotiations, whenever he was asked what he thought about the peace, he had only one answer, and that was that everything would happen according to what God wished. He added that he was convinced that God did not forsake His people, 'even though it may often appear so'. As we will see later, an essential element in Kruger's theological belief was the notion that God rewarded faithful and virtuous behaviour, and punished sinfulness, on both the individual and national levels.

When Conan Doyle wrote of the ancient theology of the Boers, almost certainly he was referring to the fact that although the Boers identified themselves as Christians, it was largely the Old Testament that comforted, informed and inspired them. Themes such as divine destiny, a nation apart, the Promised Land, a people being led through the wilderness, and the chosen people were far more prominent in the Boers' discourse and imagination than were any of the great themes of the New Testament. Many Boers would have agreed with the man who told Latrobe that Hottentots and Caffres were the 'Canaanites of this land, destined to be destroyed by the white people, who were the

Israelites of God'. It was an opinion that would have been shared quite widely, especially in frontier districts, and more so as conflict escalated.

The Boers identified so closely with their religious beliefs that they often termed themselves Christians to differentiate themselves from the black African and copper-coloured heathens or pagans by whom they were surrounded and with whom they were continually in conflict. In fact, in the minds and language of the Boers, Christian and European/white overlapped to such an extent that they were practically interchangeable. That this perception and terminology applied long before the Boers began their great trek to the north – that is to say, that it was widespread in the colony during the early nineteenth century and probably before that – is recorded by Campbell, who, describing his visit to a mission station, wrote, 'The slaves sung as well as the people called Christians, which means, in South Africa, white people.'

In the same vein, Thomas Pringle, writing during the early 1820s and deploring the conditions in the jail at Beaufort West, wrote, 'Into this apartment were crowded about thirty human beings, of both sexes, of all ages, and of almost every hue – except white.' Pringle wrote that the 'the whites, or Christen *menschen*, as they call themselves' were seldom imprisoned, except for some very severe crime – and then they would be held in some place apart from the coloured prisoners, 'lest the Christian thief or murderer should be dishonoured by being forced to associate with his brother men of swarthy hue...'

That the Boers took their self-attribution as Christian people with them into the Transvaal is shown by Mackenzie's reference during the 1860s to the *Christen menschen* of the Transvaal. Mackenzie further elaborated on the terms that the Boers used to distinguish themselves from other groups when he explained that the Boers used the word inhabitant to mean, not Bushmen or Hottentots as one might suppose, but to refer to themselves. It is interesting that Mackenzie said that Boers applied the term *volk* to all coloured people, and never to white persons. However, by the early twentieth century, the term *volk* was a self-ascribed term to describe white Afrikaans-speakers.

Two of the great components of the Boer world view were Protestantism (specifically Calvinism) and republicanism. Both derived from the Dutch experiences during the sixteenth and seventeenth centuries when the northern provinces of the Netherlands freed themselves from Spanish rule. At the Cape, the arrival of the Huguenots, who had suffered and had been cruelly persecuted for their faith, fortified loyalty and devotion to the Protestant cause amongst the Europeans there. Moreover, the Huguenots' suffering under a Catholic monarchy in France resonated with the experiences of the Dutch in their resistance to colonisation and oppression by Catholic Spain. A further bond between the earliest free burghers and the Huguenots was the fact that both groups were not only Protestants but were also Calvinists.

Three Calvinist teachings were highly influential in Boer culture as it developed from the mid-seventeenth century through to the late nineteenth century. In fact, they continued to be prevalent in Afrikaner nationalism (which can be regarded as the heir to Krugerism or Transvaal Boerism) during most of the twentieth century. The first of these is often called the doctrine of particular election. This is the teaching that some people are chosen by God for salvation. Therefore, others are not chosen, and it is easy to see how this transforms into notions of the chosen people, of a *volk* or nation with a divine purpose. These concepts inform large parts of the Old Testament which, with its narratives of a wandering people, of delivery from overwhelming dangers by divine hand, of defeating the heathens to claim a Promised Land, and of keeping faith and maintaining group and territorial boundaries in the face of heathens and external pressures, was the part of the Bible that found especial resonance with many Boers.

For instance, they would have responded fervently to the following Biblical passage from the Book of Deuteronomy:

> A wandering Aramean was my father, and he went down into Egypt, and sojourned there, few in number; and he became there a nation, great, mighty, and populous. And the Egyptians dealt ill

with us, and afflicted us, and laid upon us hard bondage. And we cried unto the Lord, the God of our fathers, and the Lord heard our voice, and saw our affliction, and our toil, and our oppression. And the Lord brought us forth out of Egypt with a mighty hand, and with an outstretched arm, and with great terribleness, and with signs, and with wonders. And He hath brought us into this place, and hath given us this land, a land flowing with milk and honey.

Ironically, this type of text, with its call of 'Let my people go!' was also the basis for liberation theology during the twentieth century. This was the theology that underpinned struggles for human and civil rights, such as the civil rights movement in the USA, struggles against oppression in South America and freedom struggles in Southern Africa.

Mackenzie depicted the role of religion as a strengthening and legitimising factor in Boer ideology when he wrote that the frontier Boer (he was referring to the Transvaal Boers) preferred the Old to the New Testament. He continued by saying that the Boers felt at home among the wars of the Israelites with the doomed inhabitants of the Promised Land and that they had persuaded themselves that they were God's chosen people, while 'the blacks are the wicked and condemned Canaanites over whose heads the Divine anger lowers continually'. As an example, said Mackenzie, a Boer would compare the 'heathen' casualties with the 'Christian' casualties. He also noted that the Boers always had services of worship when in the laager or camp, and that 'in their prayers the language of the heroes of the Old Testament is freely appropriated: they are God's people and their enemies are his enemies'.

The second influential teaching of Calvinism was that the Bible is composed of texts that are divinely ordained to reveal God's nature and purpose. In other words, the Bible was, literally, believed to be God's Word. This was integrated with the idea that the Word of God is primary and decisive. We have seen an example of this in Stanley's account of a debate in the *Volksraad*, where he mockingly recounted how parliamentary debates were decided by reference to Isaiah, the Old Testament prophet. Of course, Stanley would mock: he was a much-travelled journalist and a hardbitten imperialist who, moreover, did not seem to have much religious belief. However, if the *Volksraad* members happened to hear about Stanley's mockery, they would probably have considered Stanley to be misled or even a heathen who, sadly for him, was a lost soul who did not acknowledge God's authority and guidance.

The third influential teaching was that the preacher, as expounder of the Word of God, had a special authority and status. This followed from the belief in the authority of Scripture, and it reinforced the authoritarian and conservative nature of Boer society. Furthermore, the authority of the preacher (*dominee*) was strengthened by the fact that he was often the only educated person in the community. In nineteenth-century South Africa, and particularly in the Boer republics, access to formal education at any level was severely limited. Although there were some high schools and colleges in the colony, there were none in the Transvaal. The first director of education in the ZAR was only appointed in 1883 (he was a *dominee* in the Dutch Reformed Church and was recruited in the Cape Colony), which was less than twenty years before the republic ceased to exist. As the director resigned only six years after being appointed, and as the ZAR was chronically short of money for most of its existence, it is unlikely that much was achieved in the realm of formal education. The result was that the few educated persons had a great influence on opinion and public discourse; and the educated men who were closest to communities were usually the preachers whose main duty was to expound the Word of God, and whose main concern was to keep the flock faithful and observant.

A notable case of a *dominee* rising to high position in public life was that of Thomas Francois Burghers, who was born and raised in the Graaff-Reinet district, was educated as a theologian at Utrecht in the Netherlands, and then served as the minister of the Dutch Reformed Church in Hanover in the Cape Colony. Believing that they lacked suitable candidates for the presidency, leading citizens in the Transvaal invited burghers to stand for election in 1872. He did so and, after winning the election by a considerable majority, served as president for five years until, by then highly unpopular, he retired from political life in 1877, at the time when the British annexed the Transvaal.

Also, in view of the respect accorded to *dominees*, and the leadership that they exercised, it was no coincidence that François Malan, the first prime minister of the Afrikaner-supported National Party that came to power in South Africa in 1948, was a minister in the Dutch Reformed Church and had a doctorate in divinity.

Many senior officials in the ZAR were recruited from outside its borders because of the dearth of competent, educated local people. Jan Smuts, who was born and raised in the Cape Colony, was one such educated import who served the ZAR in an official capacity, although he was not strictly an import because he was already resident in the ZAR when he was appointed as state attorney of the Republic. Chief among the influential imports was Willem Johannes Leyds, a Dutchman who held the positions of state attorney and then state secretary. Kruger appointed Leyds after the two met while Kruger, as president of the ZAR, was on a diplomatic mission in Europe. Through Leyds, other educated Dutchmen with professional training and skills were appointed to various positions in the ZAR.

Leyds was also the prime mover in planning and arranging the construction of the railway line between the ZAR and Lourenço Marques (now Maputo) in the Portuguese colony of Mozambique. The railway was constructed and operated by the *Nederlandsch-Zuid-Afrikaansche Spoorwegmaatschappij* (Dutch-South African Railway Company) and at the time of the Anglo-Boer War, about half of its approximately 3,000 employees were from the Netherlands. This reflection of the dearth of educated and skilled people among the burghers of the ZAR is a reminder that right up to the time of the Anglo-Boer War, the large majority of burghers lived and worked on the land, learned to read and write at home and not at school, and learned their life skills on the spot from their parents, family members and neighbours.

To be a burgher or full citisen of the ZAR, one had to be a white person, and a member of the Dutch Reformed Church or of a related Calvinist church; to be a member of these churches was to have almost unquestioning faith in the authority of Scripture as well as in the persons who expounded it, namely the pastors; and the pastor or *dominee* was usually the most educated person in a community (probably the only person with much formal education) and thus an opinion-former and leader in many spheres beyond the purely religious ones.

Another dominant characteristic of the Transvaal Boers was their almost instinctive adherence to republican values and practices. The origins of this tendency are complex and interlinked; in part, they developed during the Dutch struggle for independence from Spain and from the political structures that flowed from that. The Huguenots reinforced and developed republican values and practices, based on their experiences during the time that they were oppressed by the French monarchy. However, probably the greatest influence on Boer republicanism was the teachings of Calvin, who is widely regarded as having had a significant and formative influence on both Western democracy and republicanism. In fact, in Calvinist churches, democracy extended all the way to local church level, with each congregation electing its own officers and conducting its own affairs. As can be expected, with religion and the church so central to the culture, the principles that applied in ecclesiastical affairs also informed the political views of the members of the churches.

Democratic and republican habits were strengthened by the conditions under which the early *trekboers* (that is, the free burghers who moved into the interior with their wagons and flocks) lived as they moved further and further away from the settled districts near Cape Town. While they were trekking to find new grazing space in the interior of the country, they also put both space and personal distance between themselves and the authority of the VOC officials at the Cape, whom they regarded as intrusive, corrupt and restrictive. The more they trekked and the greater the distance between themselves and Cape Town, the weaker was the authority and sway of officialdom over their lives, and the more the *trekboers* came to rely on their own resources and judgements. What Turner wrote about the American frontier was true of the Cape as well; Turner observed that 'a system of administration was not what the West demanded; it wanted land'.

4

A Rebellious People

Within a few generations, the Boers of the ever-expanding frontier had developed into a group of self-reliant people who did not pay much attention to authority, especially when authority wanted them to behave in ways that conflicted with their habits, practices and beliefs. It was a highly individualistic society, without an inherited aristocracy or inherited wealth, in which people earned respect by their own characters and achievements. To quote Turner again,

> ...the frontier is productive of individualism. Complex society is precipitated by the wilderness into a kind of primitive organisation based on the family.

In 1795, the burghers of Swellendam and Graaff-Reinet, the colony's two most outlying districts, rebelled against the VOC by expelling their company-appointed *landdrosts* (magistrates) and declaring republics. These rebellions were short-lived because both infant republics capitulated to the new authority, when the British conquered the Cape during the same year. However, although the republics were stillborn, republicanism had not been squashed. The burghers of Graaff-Reinet rebelled again in 1799 and declared a republic. This time, the rebellion was put down by force and the ringleaders were captured and sentenced to death. However, the sentence was not carried out and the condemned men were released when the Cape returned to Dutch rule. Nothing daunted, even while the ringleaders were in prison in Cape Town, there was another republican rebellion in Graaff-Reinet in 1801. This ended peacefully after conciliation.

Writing during the first decade of the nineteenth century, during the same period that these rebellions occurred, Lichtenstein provided insights into the fractious natures of the colonists, their hostile relationship with the indigenous people and the difficulties faced by the administration. Lichtenstein wrote, 'Fresh instances of disobedience to the government were constantly breaking out among the inhabitants', which meant that the authorities often had to send commissioners into distant regions to settle the disputes and establish boundaries. One of the main jobs of these commissioners and of new *drosdties* (seats of *landdrosts*, or magistrates) was 'to regulate the relations between the colonists on the northern boundary, and the wandering Bosjesmans of that neighbourhood, and to watch particularly over the behaviour of each party towards the other'. Although Lichtenstein was writing about the situation in the Roggeveld and Bokkeveld districts, about 300 to 400 kilometres north of Cape Town, his words applied equally well to other parts of the colonial frontier. In fact, as seen by the fact that burghers in the Graaff-Reinet area had rebelled twice within the space of a few years, separatist sentiments seemed to increase with greater distance from Cape Town.

It was not only on the frontier that revolutionary ideas were to be found: recalling the situation in the Cape Town-Stellenbosch region during his youth at the end of the eighteenth century, Borcherds wrote, 'As a rule, the times were unsettled. There was no lack of people who sympathized in the rage for revolution which disturbed the greater part of Europe.' He observed that because of the violence with which various parties held their views, and because the population was so mixed, 'consisting of free men and slaves. Christians, Heathens, and Mohammedans, natives and foreigners, a singular and motley compound of races in short', it was very likely that 'commotions would arise of a serious and dangerous nature'.

Of all the rebellions by the frontier Boers, Slagtersnek was the most notorious and had the furthest-reaching consequences. In fact, it is often listed amongst the prime causes of the Great Trek. I will follow

Pringle's narrative in outlining the course of this rebellion, mainly because he was close to the event in both time and space. Not only did he encounter Boer survivors of the event only five years after it happened, but he records that several of his neighbours were closely involved in the rebellion.

Pringle began his account by saying that during 1814, a Hottentot named Booy complained to the magistrate at Cradock about the oppressive conduct of Frederick Bezuidenhout, a Boer who lived at Bavian's River.[2] Booy had been in the service of Bezuidenhout for several years, but when the term of his contract expired, Bezuidenhout not only refused to allow him to leave, but also would not allow him to remove 'what little property he had on the place'. The local field cornet investigated and found that Booy's complaint was justified. Even though Bezuidenhout admitted the facts, he protested that the law was an intrusion on his rights as a free burgher. He defied the magistrate and gave Booy a vicious beating, after which he ordered Booy to tell the authorities that he would treat them in the same manner if they should dare to enter his property to recover Booy's possessions.

Pringle explained Bezuidenhout's conduct by saying that the law that gave rights to Hottentots had only been promulgated quite recently and was applied very irregularly on the frontier. In fact, said Pringle, Bezuidenhout and his comrades resided on a 'wild and secluded part of the frontier', where colonial legislation only reached them by hearsay, and where they regarded such terms as the 'rights of the natives' with contempt. Nevertheless, the law was the law, and the field cornet summoned Bezuidenhout to appear in court. When Bezuidenhout refused to appear, the circuit court judges sentenced him to imprisonment for contempt of court. Once again, Bezuidenhout refused to comply with the order of the court.

This act of defiance demanded action; as Pringle related, 'It now became necessary to act with vigour, or else to expose the laws and courts of justice to the utter contempt of the colonists.' Recognising the determined and defiant nature of the man with whom he had to deal, the sheriff took a party of soldiers with him when he went to arrest Bezuidenhout. However, Bezuidenhout had prepared for a defiant stand and took refuge in a cave under a huge rock overhanging the river, where he had hidden 'a large quantity of powder and ball, together with a supply of provisions, to stand a siege'. From this protected position, along with two young men who lived with him, he began to shoot at the party that had come to arrest him.

After an exchange of fire, one of the Hottentot soldiers killed Bezuidenhout with a rifle shot. Both the death and the fact that a non-European soldier was involved, infuriated many of the frontier Boers. When many of them gathered for the funeral, there were inflammatory speeches and several of the 'colonial patriots' (as Pringle termed them) took a solemn oath over the corpse of Bezuidenhout to revenge his death.

Led by a man named Prinsloo, the disaffected Boers tried to get Gaika, the premier chief of the neighbouring Xhosa-speaking tribes, to join their insurrection. Pringle considered that this event was another of the republican rebellions when he wrote that the men were encouraged and inflamed by the memory of what had happened at the turn of the century. In fact, said Pringle, the rebellious Boers hoped that they might achieve 'their entire independence of the English government'.

The course of this rebellion did not run smoothly. Gaika did not respond positively and, when the plot was discovered, Prinsloo was arrested and jailed. In addition, the *landdrost* of Graaff-Reinet convinced most of the burghers of the frontier areas to the north and north-east of Graaff-Reinet to stay out of the insurrection. As a result, the rebel party consisted of only about sixty men. In Pringle's opinion, most of them were hot-headed young men who were too young and inexperienced to appreciate the might of the forces that they opposed. Nor did they have the means to succeed in their plans.

A confrontation between the rebels and a force that consisted of soldiers and loyal burgher militia was followed by negotiations, after which all but five of the rebels surrendered. Of the five, four were pursued and arrested. This left only Hans Bezuidenhout, the brother of the deceased Frederick, at large. He took refuge in a protected position and shot and killed a soldier who approached him. His wife and fourteen-year-old son loaded the seven muskets at hand, which he fired at the soldiers as fast as he received them. Pringle portrays the wife as an Amazon who encouraged her husband by calling out, 'Let us never be taken alive! Let us die here together!' In the exchange of fire, Bezuidenhout was killed and, says Pringle, his wife fainted from exertion. He does not say what happened to the wife and son later.

The sequel of the affair was that thirty-nine of the rebels were convicted, of whom five were condemned to death, one to transportation and the rest to minor punishments. When the death sentence was carried out on 9 March 1816, at the place that is now called Slagtersnek, their comrades were compelled to witness the executions.

Pringle does not mention two aspects of the rebellion that further inflamed Boer feelings. The first was that the gallows beam broke and all five condemned men had to wait for a new beam to be found and erected. The whole sequence of events was witnessed by friends, family members and comrades of the deceased, many of whom wept and pleaded for mercy during the time that they were waiting for the condemned men to be strung up again. The second factor was that many of the Boers deeply resented the fact that Hottentot (that is, non-European) soldiers had been used against them.

Reitz, writing with passion on the eve of the outbreak of the Anglo-Boer War, described this event and its consequences as follows:

> six of the Boers were half hung up in the most inhuman way in the compulsory presence of their wives and children. Their death was truly horrible, for the gallows broke down before the end came; but they were again hoisted up in the agony of dying and strangled to death in the murderous tragedy of Slachter's Nek.

He concluded that this event (he called it 'a tragedy of horror') produced a gulf between Briton and Boer which lasted until the time that he was writing, about eighty-five years later.

On the other hand, Pringle wrote that in his acquaintance with many of the people who had been involved in the rebellion, he 'found them very submissive subjects to the government about the aftermath of the rebellion'. He named the former rebels as 'Erasmus, Prinslo, Vandernest, Bezuidenhout, Labuscagne, Engelbrecht, Bothma, Klopper, Malan, De Klerk, Van Dyk, etc.' When he wrote those words, Pringle was not to know that within about ten years, many of these submissive subjects would be trekking northwards to escape from British rule. With them, among their many grievances, they would carry their resentment at the affair of Slagtersnek, which fortified their determination to live free of any authority but their own.

5

Identity and Expansion

As we have seen, the Boers of the early nineteenth century were descended directly from the VOC's free burghers of the late seventeenth century who, although they were predominantly Dutch, had a strong overlay of the blood and culture of French Hugenots as well as of immigrants from other European countries. These Boers seem always to have referred themselves as burghers to distinguish themselves from other groups. For instance, in his memoirs Paul Kruger said, 'Other burghers left their home at the same time as my parents and were also encamped near the Caledon River.' (He was describing how, when he was ten years of age, his family was among the frontier Boers who left the colony as forerunners of what soon became the Great Trek.) Later, a fully fledged, enfranchised citizen of the Transvaal (ZAR) was routinely referred to as a burgher, as in these quotations from Kruger's memoirs:

> I set out again, and, accompanied by only one burgher...
> A burgher, called Paul de Beer, who spoke English well, carried the message.
> A considerable number of the burghers refused to pay [the tax].

Although nowadays, in modern Afrikaans, burgher simply means citizen and does not have any specific cultural, racial or linguistic associations, in South Africa during the nineteenth century the word had a much more restricted meaning. Borcherds, who grew up under Dutch rule in the Cape, wrote that when he reached sixteen years of age, he was officially enrolled as a burgher and 'his name was to be mentioned amongst those who could be called upon for the service of the State, and enlisted in the militia bodies destined for the protection and defence of home and hearth'.

Of course, there was more to it than being liable for military service: the contexts make it clear that to be a burgher was to be of European origin, to be accepted as white rather than non-white, to be Dutch-speaking, and to be a member either of the Dutch Reformed Church or of a related church that observed the Calvinist creed, such as the Dopper Church of which Paul Kruger was a member. By the mid-nineteenth century, it also seems to have been further restricted in meaning, referring only to the enfranchised inhabitants of the two Boer republics – that is, the Transvaal and the Orange Free State. In other words, it looks as if burgher was not applied to Boers (Pringle's Dutch-Africans) who resided in the British colonies of the Cape and Natal.

During the Middle Ages in Europe, the term burgher referred to a class of citizens in some European towns who, because of their wealth and skills, and often their membership of influential guilds, managed to secure certain rights and privileges, such as election to town councils, together with freedom of movement and property. With these rights and responsibilities, medieval burghers were elevated above ordinary people. However, it seems that later, when parts of the Netherlands were liberated from Spanish rule, the meaning of burgher was broadened or democratised to describe any inhabitant of the newly free regions. As such, the term had connotations of independence and freedom from servitude. Certainly, the first free burghers at the Cape were not called that because of their wealth or social standing. They were called burghers simply because they were citizens of the free, Dutch state.

It also appears that in the Cape Colony, among the Boers, the early connotation of burgher as free citizen of a republic held sway through two and a half centuries, from the time of the first free burghers until the end of the nineteenth century. So, when the frontier Boers in the Cape Colony termed themselves burghers, although they were subject to British control and therefore were not actually self-governing, they were implying that they identified themselves as a cohesive group with a shared history of valuing independence and republican self-government.

As the free burghers became more numerous, and as land closer to the Cape became scarcer, the burghers began to move further into the interior. For transportation, these *trekboers* used wagons drawn by oxen. Wagons were being built at the Cape well before the end of the seventeenth century, as can be seen from the fact that the Hugenots, who arrived in 1688, settled in an area that was already called Wagon Makers Valley (*Wamakersvallei*).

Many writers commented favourably on the structure and durability of the South African wagons. For instance, Moodie wrote that he admired 'the light and elegant construction' of the wagons. He stated that they were made of the lightest and most durable wood that could be found and were constructed in such a manner that they had sufficient flexibility to go over the roughest and most uneven terrain 'which would overturn any English wagon'. Early in the history of the free burghers, the twin shafts of the typical European cart gave way to the single shaft, or *disselboom*, of the South African ox wagon.

Although the wagons developed from European technology, the oxen were indigenous. They were the *sanga* breed, of which the indigenous Khoi had large herds. In time, these animals developed into the well-known Afrikaner cattle, with their characteristic red hides, humps and sweeping horns. In fact, it is likely that the burghers imitated the Khoi practice of using oxen as draught animals to carry loads as well as riders. The Khoi practice is graphically depicted in the painting by Samuel Daniell (1805) titled *Kora-Khokhoi preparing to move*, in which a huge, red, humpbacked ox with sweeping horns stands loaded with mats, bundles, weapons, hut poles and household implements while its owners complete the process of breaking camp. That the Khoi were not easily separated from their oxen is shown by a comment by Campbell who, writing in about 1815, observed of the

Hottentot soldiers in British service who escorted him through the recently conquered Zuurveld that he was amused to see the men riding upon the oxen with their guns.

Soon, the ox wagon became essential to the life of the colonists, whether for carrying produce and materials, for transporting people and possessions while they were trekking in search of new grazing lands, for semi-permanent or permanent accommodation, or even for protection in the *laager* formation. In fact, for many of the frontier Boers, the wagon provided more of a home than did an earthbound dwelling; writing during the early nineteenth century, Philip said this about the nomadic habits of many Boers:

> As their flocks and herds are very extensive, amounting frequently from five thousand to seven thousand, including horned cattle, sheep, and goats, it becomes necessary for them, in those parched parts of the country, to move constantly in search of pasturage. For two-thirds of the year, they are consequently from home, living in wagons, like the ancient Scythians.

And so, in their wagons drawn by spans of oxen, accompanied by family members, servants, slaves, herds, and flocks, the *trekboers* pressed onward into the interior, leaving behind the settled districts, going where they wanted to, settling where they chose, and killing or enslaving anyone who tried to prevent them from doing so. Today many Westerners look back on their societies' colonial and imperial pasts with surprise and even with disdain. How, they ask, could people have invaded other people's territories (usually without cause or provocation), how could they subdue and/or kill and/or enslave the inhabitants, seize their lands and property, import colonists to occupy the territories, and foist their foreign culture and religion on the people that they had subjugated? How could Westerners have had such an implacable belief in the superiority of their culture and beliefs, and how could they have been so disdainful and contemptuous of the indigenous cultures that they encountered?

These questions have been asked countless times, and analyses and answers have been provided in thousands, if not in scores of thousands, of books and articles, as well as in productions in other types of media. Whatever the reasons, during the whole of the time that Western countries were engaged in exploration and expansion on other continents, from about the middle of the sixteenth century until the mid-twentieth century, few voices were raised in opposition, or expressed serious reservations about the attitudes and actions that underlay imperialism and colonialism. Even where the injuries and damages were acknowledged, usually they were shrugged off regretfully as collateral damage in the great imperial project. This also applied to the Dutch colonial project at the Cape, where there is little evidence of contemporary reflections on the rights and property of the indigenous people. On the contrary, it was taken for granted that Europeans had the right to take what they wanted, and to destroy or enslave anybody who tried to prevent them from doing so. The few dissenting voices came from newcomers such as Philip and Pringle, as well as some travelling visitors, who had receptive audiences at home in Britain but were generally decried in the colony.

The colonists' sensibilities and consciences were conditioned by preconceptions about the inhabitants that they conquered and dispossessed, and about the territories that they occupied. One illusion was that Europeans were penetrating *terra nullius* (nobody's land), which meant that the colonised land was regarded as effectively unoccupied and unowned, despite clear proof to the contrary. A reserve position on *terra nullius* was that although the territories were occupied, the inhabitants were not sovereign nations and therefore should not be recognised as legitimate owners of the land.

The second preconception was based on the belief in a hierarchy of civilisation, which allowed superior rights to those who were clearly more advanced. This is how Lichtenstein expresses the notion of a hierarchy:

> There is not perhaps any class of savages upon the earth that lead lives so near those of the brutes as the *Bosjesmans* [Bushmen]; none

perhaps who are sunk so low, who are so unimportant in the scale of existence; whose wants, whose cares, and whose joys, are so low in their nature; and who are consequently so little capable of cultivation.

To this, he added that Bushmen more resembled apes than humans. Pursuing his thesis that people who were closer to Europeans were more advanced, Lichtenstein also wrote that during their travels near the Orange River, which was then beyond the borders of the colony, he and his companions visited a settlement that was occupied by Bastards (people of mixed ancestry) and Bushmen. He commented that the former lived in large clean huts, and were clothed in linen or woollen cloth, while the latter lived in 'dirty *pandoks* and had skins thrown over them'. (*Pandok* was a derogative term for a flimsy, insubstantial hut.) Lichtenstein meant that people with some proportion of European ancestry were superior to those without any.

Moodie, who wrote during the 1830s, expressed a similar opinion about a hierarchy of cultures when he described Khoi people as providing a 'deplorable and degrading picture of human nature' and occupying a position 'beneath the more favoured race'.

Writing about fifty years later and expressing the same view, Aylward, after complaining that white settlers in the eastern Cape had to use 'the tongue of the inferior race', that is, isiXhosa, when communicating with their African neighbours, then explained, 'By inferior, I here mean nothing more than lower in the ranks of civilisation.'

Almost a century after Lichtenstein, Massie wrote in the same vein that the Bushmen were 'pigmies in stature, and very low down in the scale of civilisation'. Above them, he placed the Hottentots, who were 'vastly superior in every way to the Bushmen'.

At about the same time, towards the end of the nineteenth century, the historian George McCall Theal also espoused the concept of a cline of civilisation when he wrote about the early years of the nineteenth century as follows:

At this time, the country along the Orange was infested by Griqua and Korana marauders... They belonged to the Hottentot race, a people physically inferior to the Basuto, and below them in civilisation.

Here, Theal was ranking people of mixed ancestry below pure Africans such as the Basuto.

Lichtenstein had a novel suggestion for raising the Bushmen from their savage condition to something approaching a civilised state. He wrote to the governor at the Cape to suggest that, rather than being killed, the Bushmen should be imprisoned, perhaps on Robben Island in the sea off Cape Town. There they could do moderate work, the profits of which might pay for the expenses of their imprisonment. Through this experience, they would 'be led to adopt more active and civilised lives'. Finally, as a reward for good behaviour, 'the best might gradually be restored to liberty, and allowed to return home, where they might introduce something like civilisation among their countrymen'. In fact, many Bushmen were captured and imprisoned on Robben Island and at the Breakwater Convict Station in Cape Town, where they did hard labour on the harbour works. However, the aim was not to civilise them, but to punish them.

It appears that the conflict between colonists and Bushmen continued until at least the third quarter of the nineteenth century. For instance, between the years 1857 and 1875, the linguist Wilhelm Bleek used Bushmen prisoners from both aforementioned prisons as informants in his ground-breaking attempts to record and describe Bushmen languages. The prisoners came from the Burghersdorp, Colesberg and Kenhardt regions, which are all located in the drier northern and north-eastern parts of the colony. Although these districts were located well within the borders of the colony by that time, it appears that the struggle between colonists and Bushmen, which was so prevalent on the expanding frontier, continued even under more settled conditions.

6

Appropriation and Extermination

When the Dutch established their settlement at the Cape in 1652, the south-western regions of Africa were occupied by the Khoi. The Khoi were pastoralists with large herds of cattle and sheep and, with their draught oxen and easily dismantled housing, were relatively nomadic. They are also called the Khoikhoi, while many colonists called them Hottentots, which probably referred to the 'click' sounds in their language. In time, Hottentot came to be a derogatory term that was used by whites to indicate inferiority and express disdain.

Archaeological evidence suggests that the first Khoi bands entered the northern parts of Southern Africa about 1,500 years before the Dutch settled at the Cape. It also suggests that they were not pastoralists originally, but that they got their cattle and sheep from the Bantu tribes, who were also moving into the region. Whatever the case, all the records show that the Khoi were pastoralists with large herds when Europeans first encountered them.

However, the Khoi were not the first inhabitants of southern Africa; that distinction belongs to the San, who are also called Bushmen.[3] Archaeologists say that the San presence in the region is very ancient, and possibly even reaches back to the very origins of humankind. When the Dutch settled at the Cape, the hunter-gatherer San were already under pressure from the Khoi in the west and south of southern Africa, and from the advancing Bantu-speaking groups in the north and the east.

The nature of the relationship between the Khoi and the San is disputed and is difficult to disentangle. It is easy to hypothesise a common origin, because they both spoke languages with click sounds and because they were similar in appearance. In addition, of course, they both occupied the same stretches of territory. Some observers claim that the two were essentially of the same race and origin, with the main distinction – namely, hunter-gatherer versus pastoralist – arising because the Khoi migrated into the region much later, learning pastoral habits and getting sheep and cattle, from the migrating Bantu.

Whatever the relationship between the two groups, by the early decades of the nineteenth century, European writers were making a clear distinction between Khoi and San. Ironically, by that time, the Khoi, who were referred to as Hottentots in texts, had almost ceased to exist as an independent people. Those who had survived the scourge of smallpox and the assaults of the Boer commandos were serving as indentured labourers on the farms. Indentured usually meant that, in effect, they were slaves; in fact, Theal referred unambiguously to the Hottentot slaves of the frontier Boers, while Pringle showed that the relationship was more complex but no less dire when he wrote that although the law did not allow Hottentots to be sold from owner to owner, they were not able to decide freely where and for whom they would work, and were 'reduced to a condition of degrading, grinding, and hopeless bondage, in some respects even more intolerable than colonial slavery of the ordinary description'.

Writing about ten years earlier, during the second decade of the nineteenth century, Latrobe expressed the same opinion when he stated that the degradation into which the Hottentot nation had sunk was caused by the colonists, who had forced the Khoi into the most abject servitude. In their current condition, said Latrobe, they were 'far worse treated than purchased slaves', because (echoing a common opinion) slaves were often more valued than indentured Hottentots.

Under the influence of Enlightenment pressure at home, after the British appropriated the Cape in 1806, various governors tried to ameliorate the bondage that had been imposed on the Hottentots. It was under the influence of one of these attempts, as we have seen, that the Hottentot man named Booy, who was involved in the event that triggered the Slagtersnek incident, was emboldened to complain that his former master, Frederick Bezuidenhout, had appropriated some of his possessions. Bezuidenhout, who was accustomed to the former dispensation, considered that a slave could not claim anything as his own. He was defying the new law that attempted to regularise relations between servants and masters because, as Pringle said, Bezuidenhout considered the law to be a violation of his rights. From this irreconcilable opposition between ancient, entrenched ideas about the ordained relationship between master and slave, between colonist and indigene, and new ideas about the rights of man, came Booy's assertion that he could walk free and take his belongings with him. From that followed Bezuidenhout's indignation and his defiance of a law whose premises he could not comprehend, but whose effects he understood well enough; and from that followed Slagtersnek, and all its resentments and consequences.

The eastwards and north-eastwards movements of the *trekboers* had such devastating effects on the Khoi that hardly any independent communities remained by the early decades of the nineteenth century. The devastation caused by the colonists, as well as smallpox epidemics, almost completely wiped out the Khoi, while the San or Bushmen were driven further and further into arid and inhospitable parts of the subcontinent. Lichtenstein (1815) observed that the Bushmen were in a desperate situation because, although there were some areas, such as the banks of the Orange River, where they could find the necessities of life, in other places 'which are deficient in game, in ants, in locusts, and in bulbs, they are often in a deplorable situation'. The result, he said, was that they wasted away and were 'the leanest, most wretched figures imaginable'. The inevitable result, wrote Lichtenstein, was that the Bushmen resorted to robbing the colonists: and, he asked, could they be blamed, because they had no possessions but their bows and arrows, and had no other means of getting sustenance?

Lichtenstein depicted the unremitting and savage nature of the struggle for land and survival when he wrote that different norms and values applied on the distant frontier, where the law had a feeble reach. The colonist saw no wrong in defending his property, even if he killed some of the attackers; and, asked Lichtenstein, could he be judged by the standards of more well-constituted states? Lichtenstein's conclusion was that 'the rude laws of nature must inevitably, in great measure, rule here...' In other words, being largely beyond the reach of central authority, the frontier Boers acted according to their own norms and imposed their own order and wills on the more vulnerable races.

Lichtenstein was uncomplimentary about the nomadic Boers who did not have settled domiciles 'but move about with their flocks from place to place'. He called them 'of the poorest class in the colony'; further, he wrote that even though they were often responsible for atrocities, they were able to conceal themselves and their crimes from authority. He complained that, moving about as they did, they seemed to be so divorced from human society 'that they are almost sunk to the situation of savages'. Here, Lichtenstein gave another perspective on the lives and natures of *trekboers*, who Afrikaner mythology later idealised as independent-minded, ruggedly virtuous, self-sufficient and self-determining people. However, besides describing them as almost sunk to the situation of savages, Lichtenstein suggested that they were also vicious, ruthless in pursuit of material advantages, cold-bloodedly predatory and liable to conflate justice with own advantage.

At the same time, Lichtenstein retailed a fiction that he must have heard from colonists who tried to justify their part in the brutal and violent struggle. The fiction was that the Bushmen had never occupied any of the districts that were now occupied by the colonists; consequently, the Bushmen were the aggressors and the colonists were only defending what was rightfully theirs. Lichtenstein said that at the time 'when the Europeans settled in the Roggeveld, in the Snow Mountains, in Agte-bruintjeshoogte, and other parts, there were no *Bosjesmans* there'; instead, the Bushmen were attracted to those parts by the wealth of the colonists.

Another result of these pressures on indigenous groups was that distinctions became blurred as the Khoi were dispossessed of their animals and grazing lands, and as the Bushmen were pushed back from more fertile districts, so that by the early decades of the nineteenth century, many of the people referred to as Bushmen were probably of mixed Khoi-San ancestry. In similar vein, writing during the following decade, Campbell reported that 'The Hottentots, who are the aborigines of this country, are a people nearly extinct; a few kraals [settlements] only remaining within the limits of the colony.' Ten years later, Pringle described the process of destruction by saying that the Khoi had either been driven into the most desolate regions, or had been assimilated, or had been extirpated. After consulting the colonial records in Cape Town, he reckoned that the process had been going on for at least 120 years. As Pringle was writing during the mid-1820s, he dated the beginning of the conflict to about 1700, or less than fifty years after the Dutch established the settlement at the Cape.

The extermination of Hottentot culture and identity was so comprehensive that, as Backhouse noted while visiting the south-western Cape during the late 1830s, '[Dutch] has become the mother-tongue of the Hottentots of this part of the Colony, many of whom know little or nothing of the native language of their ancestors.' This comment agreed with Lichtenstein's observation, a generation or more earlier, about the loss of indigenous language when he wrote that 'In the colony, and in the service of the Europeans, very few Hottentots are to be found who are not able to speak the Dutch language, or who speak their own language pure and entire.' It was his opinion that only beyond the borders of the colony were there groups who still spoke the indigenous languages as had been done before the arrival of the Europeans. As sociolinguists know, loss of an original language is a sure indication of the death of culture and identity.

The pressures on the indigenous races gave rise to mixed-race groups such as the Griquas and the Oorlams, who adopted European methods and technology but lived beyond the frontiers of the colony.

With their land hunger and raids for cattle and sheep, as well as for slaves, these groups caused further disturbances, so that tsunami-like waves of disruption spread ever outwards until they dissipated in the distant interior. As early as the first decade of the nineteenth century, when writing about his experiences on a journey beyond the borders of the colony, Borcherds said that he heard 'the most fearful stories of cruelties committed by these banditti upon the Namaquas, of whom many had been murdered'. (The Namaqua would have been a group of original Khoi people.) Borcherds continued by relating some of the atrocities that had been committed by the outcast bandits:

> Women and children were tied to trees and, after being ill-treated, killed, and whole communities had been robbed of their cattle; so that these inoffensive tribes, not able to defend themselves with their inferior weapon, the spear, were now wandering about in a state of want and privation, many perishing from hunger.

Writing of his experiences at about the same time, Lichtenstein described these marginalised people as 'children of the Hottentot women, in whose veins Christian blood often flowed', and noted that in earlier days, they often established themselves in relatively prosperous and settled conditions in frontier areas such as the lower Bokkeveld. However, said Lichtenstein, this ended when the growing population of the colony expanded outward, with new generations of colonists looking for more land for themselves. Driven away from districts where they could make a settled living, the Bastard Hottentots retreated further and further into the arid regions until they eventually ended up seeking refuge on the banks of the Orange River and beyond.

Describing the situation about twenty years later, Pringle put it like this:

> And thus on the outskirts of our ever-advancing frontier, numerous wandering hordes of destitute and desperate savages – the South-African 'Children of the Mist'[4] – have been constantly found in a state of precarious truce, or of bitter hostility with the colonists.

Lichtenstein also provided graphic descriptions of the predatory habits of some of the bands who lived beyond the northern frontier of the colony near the Great (or Orange) River. For instance, he described the activities of a man called Danster, who led a band that once was allied with the Afrikaner clan. (The Afrikaners were a group of mixed-race ancestry who migrated into present-day southern Namibia during the late eighteenth century.) Lichtenstein said that Danster talked so freely and easily about the raids and murders in which he had been involved, and which he was planning to do, that it horrified him and his fellow travellers. Lichtenstein also recorded that Danster told him about the predatory activities of a band of Europeans who, operating beyond the frontier, lived entirely by hunting and plunder; this group consisted of renegade colonists, together with deserters from the British and Dutch armies. These marginalised and outcast groups had well established contacts with the colonists and carried on a contraband trade for powder and fire-arms in exchange for horned-cattle, elephants' teeth, ostrich feathers, and the hides of animals.

In passing, it is both amusing and pertinent to note Moodie's account of how the mixed races came about. Moodie, a visitor from Britain who cast a sardonic eye over much that he saw in the colony, wrote, 'It may seem somewhat extraordinary to Europeans, but it is nevertheless true, that the colonists, both Dutch and English, are very partial to the female Hottentots.' Of course, said Moodie, the colonists concealed their fancies from their wives, by pretending to be disgusted by Hottentot women. Moodie continued by saying, 'The colonial female Hottentots, indeed, are often strikingly elegant in their proportions, and they have all that lightness, and ease in their motions for which all savages are remarkable.' It was no wonder, wrote Moodie, that 'they are often preferred to the clumsy, torpid, and insensible Dutchwomen, with their stony eyes and jealous domineering manners.' Here, as on a number of other occasions in his book, Moodie showed that he, too, was susceptible to the charms of Hottentot women.

7

The Gonaquas and Stuurman

Writing during the mid-1820s, Thompson's account of the fate of the Gonaqua Hottentots is illuminating because it provides a more detailed view of how Khoi groups were treated and how it affected them. At some unspecified time, but probably until no later than the first half of the eighteenth century, the Gonaqua tribe occupied the land between Algoa Bay and the Bashee (Mbashe) River, a stretch of about 450 kilometres along the coast, ranging from west of present-day Port Elizabeth to a point about 150 kilometres beyond present-day East London. Thompson got these details from an old man of Gonaqua background who spoke about the time when, during his own lifetime, their tribal territory stretched from Algoa Bay to the Fish River. It appears that the Gonaquas were subjected to pressures from two sides because, if we estimate the man to have been about sixty years of age when he spoke to Thompson, then Gonaqua tribal land stretched as far eastwards as the Fish River during the mid-1770s. As the Bashee River, the earliest known boundary of the Gonaquas' territory, is about 250 kilometres east of the Fish River, this suggests that at some before the mid-1770s, the Gonaqua people would have retreated westward, from the Bashee River to the Fish River.

This was confirmed by another old man of Gonaqua ancestry who spoke to Andrew Smith, a British traveller, during the 1820s or 1830s. Smith reported that

> In olden days [there were]…more cattle with the Hottentots than the farmers now have. The old man says that the Hottentots and Caffers never fought; that the Hottentots kept moving west as the Caffers approached them.

Corroborating the claims, Campbell stated that he spoke to a Hottentot chief named Benedictus Platje Royters who said that all the country around present-day Port Elizabeth and Uitenhage, and also the Zuurveld, which is an extensive area east of Port Elizabeth, belonged to his grandfather. However, they had been deprived of it by the boors and Caffers.

For the Gonaqua, as for all the 'Hottentot' groups, it was an unceasing litany of woe. As seen above, during the mid-1770s, their land stretched from near present-day Port Elizabeth to the Fish River, thus extending about 200 kilometres along the coast; this was a contraction by half of the earlier, known extent of their reach. However, by the end of the second decade of the nineteenth century, the tribe had almost completely disappeared, either extirpated, in Pringle's words, or absorbed into Bushmen or Caffer/Kaffir (black-African or Bantu-speaking) communities. Some of the hapless descendants of the Gonaqua might have been serving as indentured labourers – effectively slaves – on settler farms, while others might have been relatively protected by residing on mission stations. However, as is clear from what Campbell observed during his visit to Bethelsdorp (which is now part of the urban sprawl of Port Elizabeth), residing at a mission station did not exempt an inhabitant from being pressed into service. Campbell wrote that many inhabitants of the mission station were starving because of the large number of men who were either in the service of farmers or were on active service as guides at military posts, all without pay for their work. He gave as an example that 'only two days ago, twelve men were demanded to go against the Caffres; and yesterday, fifteen men, with their pack oxen, were ordered to repair to the different military posts as guides, etc.'

Thompson summarised the situation by saying that, in his time, the tribe was extinct. The remnants were either serving on farms or had taken refuse with the Xhosa-speaking groups across the frontier. In a moving eulogy, he wrote,

Now the white men claim the entire property of the soil, and have even deprived the original possessors of the privilege of living free upon roots and game. They are accounted an inferior race, and born to servitude. They feel their degradation, but cannot escape from it...

Even though the colonists had claimed huge tracts of land and had wiped out or enslaved almost all the original inhabitants, there appeared to be no end to colonial advancement. The frontier was still expanding and there was still resistance to be overcome. Pringle recorded a sobering conversation that he had in 1821 with 'field-commandant Van Wyk, generally considered one of the most respectable men in the Cradock district', who spoke to Pringle while he and his fellow commando members were returning from active duty. Pringle wrote that Van Wyk told him that the commando members had killed more than eighty people and, in addition, 'had taken captive a considerable number of women and children, some of whom I afterwards saw at the residence of our neighbour Wentzel Coetzer, in the service of one of his sons who had been on the expedition'. This was one more instance of an old-established and widely accepted pattern on the frontier of the colony, namely that the commando members killed those who resisted and enslaved the survivors. If there were cattle and sheep to be gained, then it was all to the good.

Pringle also provided a graphic account of the life, times, and fate of a man who has been called the last Gonaqua chief. His name was David Stuurman and he lived from about 1773 until 1830. During 1803, David Stuurman, his two brothers and their followers, who seem to have been the only survivors of the Gonaqua tribe, were given a stretch of land on the Little Gamtoos River, which is close to present-day Uitenhage and Port Elizabeth. As already discussed, the extent of their tribal land had shrunk drastically. Furthermore, the tribe had completely lost its autonomy, because now it only occupied land at the pleasure of the governor at the Cape. Pringle said that, upon receiving the land, 'They then retired thither with such scanty stock of sheep and cattle as they could muster, and continued to live quietly, after the manner of their forefathers, by pasturage and hunting.'

The Gamtoos Valley near Port Elizabeth as it is today – a location well known to David Stuurman.

When his older brother died, David succeeded him as chief. However, some Boers who lived nearby were jealous of the land that the group occupied and resented the Gonaquas for having fought together with the Caffers in an insurrection against the Europeans. (This was during the Third Frontier War of 1799–1803.) Therefore, says Pringle, local Boers made numerous complaints to the civil authorities with the aim of evicting the Gonaquas and reducing them to the same state of servitude as the rest of their fellows. For seven years, their efforts were in vain. However, in 1810, when their contracts expired, two members of the Gonaqua group left the service of a nearby Boer farmer and returned to take up residence with their fellows. The farmer was affronted because he regarded all Hottentots as subservient and did not recognise contractual agreements. When some Boers went to the Gonaqua settlement to demand that the two men should be handed over, David Stuurman refused to yield them. After an armed confrontation, the Boers departed.

Not long afterwards, the local *landdrost* and some farmers managed to capture Stuurman. Pringle wrote that the rest of the party dispersed in confusion, after which they were seized by the *landdrost* and allocated as servants to neighbouring farmers. Some fled over the frontier, while a few could take refuge at the mission station of Bethelsdorp, following pleas by the missionary, Van der Kemp. The chief and his brother, together with two others, were sent to Cape Town as prisoners. There, after being tried on a charge of resisting the civil authorities, they were condemned to hard labour for life on Robben Island. Pringle also recorded that the *landdrost* requested, and was granted, ownership of the land that the group had occupied; moreover, to compound the injury, he pressed some of Stuurman's children into his service.

Latrobe, who visited the area not long afterwards, during 1815, wrote that all available land on the Gamtoos River was occupied by colonists. There was no land available for the Gonaquas, although a governor had allocated space to them. He added that although the English governors had intended to restore the site to the Gonaqas, it was 'already in possession of a farmer, though without a grant from Government'.

In 1816, Stuurman and two of his comrades escaped from Robben Island and made their way through the coastal districts of the colony – a distance of about 900 kilometres – until they reached safety amongst the Xhosa-speaking tribes across the Fish River. However, three years later, Stuurman was captured when he entered the colony, presumably to visit family members and friends. He was returned to Robben Island but, once again, he escaped. This time, he was sentenced to death. However, because of circumstances at the time of the escape, the sentence was commuted to life imprisonment and he was transported to New South Wales in 1823. He died as a convict in Sydney in 1830.

When Pringle returned to Britain during 1826, he published an account of David Stuurman's life and mistreatment. It attracted the attention of General Bourke, the lieutenant-governor at the Cape. Bourke wrote to the governor of New South Wales on behalf of David Stuurman, who was given improved conditions as a ticket of leave convict, which allowed the holder to earn wages for his own benefit.

The next recorded event in the drama occurred in 1831 when, after Bourke was appointed governor of New South Wales, Pringle corresponded with him about the matter. Bourke received the plea sympathetically and got consent for Stuurman to be repatriated to his home and family, if his return was not opposed by the Cape government. However, Stuurman died before Bourke reached New South Wales. Pringle concluded his account with these sombre words: 'Such was the fate of the last Hottentot chief who attempted to stand up for the rights of his countrymen.'

I have a special interest in the story of David Stuurman because I first read about the matter when I was living in Surry Hills, in Sydney, close to the place where Stuurman was buried after he died in the General Hospital in Sydney. Most likely, he was buried in the Devonshire Street cemetery, which seems to have been the only one (or perhaps the main one) in use in Sydney at that time – and I read about the matter and wrote these words while I was living in Devonshire Street, less than one hundred metres away from the eastern boundary of the old cemetery. In 1900, when the Central Railway Station was built on the site, remains from the cemetery were exhumed and relocated. Although careful records were kept when the reinternments were done, I could not find a record of death or burial for Stuurman when I checked sources in both the New South Wales State Library and the NSW State Archives. Nor could I find a record of reinternment. One reason might be that convicts were buried in poorly marked graves that disappeared over the years, so that there were no traces of many graves, especially the earlier ones, when the remains were moved in 1900. However, I am not an archivist, so there might be a record elsewhere. I say this with reference to the fact that, at the time that I wrote these words, there was an initiative by descendants of the Gonaqua to discover the remains of David Stuurman and return them to his country.

It is poignant to think that a man from the eastern Cape, who was born, raised, had a family, and enjoyed the company of his friends and compatriots, less than 100 kilometres from where I grew up in Port Elizabeth, should have ended his days as a prisoner in exile in a strange and foreign continent among people from distant and alien cultures. Also, apart from that I grew up in the same area as he did, I feel another connection with David Stuurman, and that is the fact that there is a room in the South End Museum in Port Elizabeth that is filled with a display about his life – and the museum is in the building in which I attended Sunday school as a boy.

It is a truism that history is written by the victors. Certainly, there are few records of the feelings and experiences of the indigenous inhabitants of the Cape Colony during the many years that they were harassed and oppressed. Year after year, members of Khoi communities had their land stolen and were pressed into servitude, robbed, denigrated and killed, with almost no relief and with no prospect of rescue or recovery in sight. Through the record of the life and fate of David Stuurman we can at least get some insights into what he must have felt as he endured implacable injustice, the theft of his land and possessions, the dispersal and enslavement of his compatriots and family members, trials that were travesties of justice, desperate conditions in prisons, the longing for freedom and self-determination, and finally banishment to a prison colony that was separated by an ocean and a continent from all that he yearned for and loved. And, always, the hopeless sense of implacable injustice must have weighed down on him until, finally and probably mercifully, he was released by death and was buried in an unknown grave in a foreign continent.

8

Colonial Borders

Leaving the Gonaqua people and their struggles on the south-eastern coast and its adjacent interior, I will turn to the equally savage conflict that took place on the northern and north-eastern fringes of the colony. Thompson gives a graphic account of these events when he reports what he had heard from an old Hottentot of between sixty and seventy years of age who said that

> he could recollect the time when few or no murders were committed by the Bushmen, especially upon the Christians. The era of bitter and bloody hostility between them commenced, according to his account, about fifty years ago...

Thompson's informant said that the conflict began because of an incident near the Zak River[5] when some Bushmen in the service of a Boer could no longer endure his cruelties and killed him. In retaliation, wrote Thompson, a strong commando was sent into the Bushmen country, and hundreds of people were massacred to avenge the death of the farmer. (Thompson called him 'this ruffian'.) When the Bushmen rose in revolt and launched attacks on the colonists, the conflict stretched from the Kamiesberg to the Stormberg. From that time onwards, said Thompson's informant, those parts of the frontier were never at rest. Raids were followed by retaliatory attacks, killings and abductions in almost never-ending sequence.

Thompson's informant spoke of events that occurred fifty years earlier, around 1770–80, and his testimony fits well with other evidence. The reference to Kamieskroon suggests that by the mid-

1770s the *trekboers* had fanned out northward to points about 500 kilometres from Cape Town, while the reference to Stormberg suggests that the north-eastern fringe of their reach was then about 250 kilometres east of Graaff-Reinet. From Kamiesberg to Stormberg is about 1,000 kilometres as the crow flies so, if the informant was correct, the bloody encounters stretched over an arc of considerable distance. Once again, it is not certain who the Bushmen were who were involved in the conflict, but it is likely that they were original San people together with refugees from dispossessed Khoi communities, as well as people of mixed Khoi and San origin.

While most histories refer to Frontier Wars at various fixed dates during the eighteenth and early nineteenth centuries, the dates only mark especially serious or large-scale encounters. In fact, conflict between the *trekboers* and indigenous people was almost endemic throughout this period. For instance, Philip refers to a certain Commandant Nel who told him that he had been involved in thirty commandos against the Bushmen during the previous thirty-two years. This would have been during the period 1790–1825 so, according to Nel's own testimony, he had been actively involved in armed conflict on average of nearly one excursion per year. Nel further told Philip that during these expeditions, 'great numbers [of Bushmen] had been shot, and their children carried into the colony. On one of these expeditions, not less than two hundred Bushmen had been destroyed.'

Philip's reaction was to write,

> Such has been and, to a great extent, still is, the horrible warfare existing between the Christians and the natives of the northern frontier, and by which the process of extermination is still proceeding against the latter, in the same style as in the days of Barrow.

Barrow travelled in the Cape Colony during 1797–98, about thirty-five years before Philip, and his account of the vicious nature of the conflict between *trekboers* and Bushmen agreed with the accounts of later observers. Writing of his experiences while travelling from the

Cape to Graaff-Reinet via the southern reaches of the Karoo, Barrow wrote that the colonists regarded the name Bushmen with horror and detestation; they thought that they were doing a good thing by wiping out the Bushmen. He said that when he asked someone in Graaff-Reinet 'if the savages were numerous or troublesome on the road', the man replied that 'he had only shot four'. Barrow said that the man made the statement as calmly as if he had been speaking about shooting partridges. Barrow concluded by stating, somewhat sceptically, that he had heard one colonist boast about killing 300 Bushmen. That this was not an isolated occurrence or sentiment is plain from the words of Lichtenstein, who travelled in the Cape Colony during the first decade of the nineteenth century. Of a farm in the Karoo, on the then-colonial frontier north-west of Graaff-Reinet, he wrote that, 'The neighbourhood of this farm is often the theatre of terrible strifes with the Bosjesmans.' Lichtenstein also stated that the farmer told him, with indifference and with no show of emotion, that not far away, lying out on the open plain, there were some skeletons of Bushmen who had been shot by a farmer while they were stealing some of his oxen.

When one reads generalised accounts of violence and warfare, it is easy to forget that the conflicts are never over when the fighting ends. Instead, they leave deep scars on those who experience them directly, as well as on generations to come. Usually, the emotions are so aroused, and the suffering is so deep, that the depth of passions cannot be comprehended by people who were not involved or who have not had similar experiences. Some of the common effects are consuming hatred, thirst for revenge and the drive to attain future security by erecting barriers, both psychological and material, to make one's defences impregnable. To give some insights into what the ongoing violence and insecurity on the colonial frontier meant on the individual level, I have reproduced in the next few paragraphs some accounts of the suffering and dislocations that were experienced in the Colony during the long period of warfare and insecurity.

Writing of his experiences during 1803–06, Lichtenstein stated that Bushman raids would cost farmers at least five per cent of their sheep and cattle annually, while in the more exposed Snow Mountains, 'many a farmer has on a single occasion suffered such heavy losses, as to throw him several years behind hand in his circumstances'. (The Snow Mountains or Sneeuwberge are about 250 kilometres north-east of Cape Town.) Lichtenstein also recorded witnessing distress in the Roggeveld area, about 300 kilometres north of Cape Town, where, he wrote, the Bushmen had driven away more than 200 head of cattle, and a much larger number of sheep; in addition, they had murdered several herdsmen and shepherds. He observed that the situation was so insecure that the colonists had fled into arid and inhospitable parts of the Karoo in their search for security. He also reported that while he was visiting a farm where the wife was home alone because her husband and his men (Hottentots) were out searching for cattle that had been stolen by Bushmen the previous night, several wagons packed with colonists and their belongings passed by, fleeing from their homes and urging everybody to leave the Roggeveld.

Lichtenstein also provided a moving account of how an old, blind man, who Lichtenstein respected as a fellow botanist, told him about how he was deprived of all that he possessed, including his home, when he had to flee before the advancing enemy. As Lichtenstein met the man in Swellendam, and the man had fled from somewhere in the Tsitsikamma region, the incident probably took place during the Frontier War of 1799–1803, when combined Khoi and Xhosa forces pushed back the colonists as far westwards as Oudtshoorn. (As indicated earlier, this episode would have been a major reason for which revenge was later exacted on the Gonaqua tribe and David Stuurman.) According to Lichtenstein, the farm at which the blind man was living was surprised in the night by the enemy and the inhabitants, who were outnumbered, were glad to escape with their lives in the darkness. Lichtenstein continued by saying that the old blind man 'was carried away, half-led, half-dragged, to the next farm, where a wagon was obtained for pursuing the flight'. However, although his life was saved, he lost all his possessions, including his books and collection of plants. (This loss struck a chord with his fellow botanist, Lichtenstein.) In this bereft state, the old man was taken to Swellendam, where he was cared for by an old friend who 'provided him with food, lodging and clothing without ever expecting the least return'.

Writing ten years later, Campbell described the precarious situation of a Boer family in the Zuurveld, east of present-day Port Elizabeth, which was then on the eastern frontier. Campbell wrote,

> In the forenoon I rode with Major Prentice in his wagon to a boor's, a few miles distant, who was lately plundered of sheep by the Caffres. A son of his, a stout young man, lately left him from dread of being murdered by them. The family have occasion to be in constant readiness to repel any attack that may be made upon them, which undoubtedly is a most irksome situation to be in…

Later in his journey, between the Zuurveld and Graaff Reinet, Campbell came across some ruined houses and was told that some years earlier, the Boers in that area banded together and drove the *landdrost* from Graaff Reinet because 'some of his proceedings displeased them'. While they were doing this, the 'Caffres' seized the opportunity to attack their defenceless properties, destroying many houses and carrying off the cattle. (This would have happened during the rebellion of 1801.)

A few years later, Latrobe, then near Plettenberg Bay on the Tsitsikamma coast, was told about a dramatic episode that occurred about fifteen years earlier. Latrobe related that during the last invasion of the colony, a party of 'Caffres' surprised some Boers and killed five of them in cool blood. While one of the wives was begging for the life of her husband, after some discussion, the assailants suddenly seized him and cut him in pieces. Then they carried off one of the women and kept her captive for four days. During this time, they sent a message to her husband, demanding 200 rix-dollars as a ransom. However, he refused to deal with them because he thought that they were going to defraud him. During this time, the woman persisted in her pleas to be released, and eventually, they sent her home without ransom and unharmed.

Latrobe also provided another revealing account of the insecurities that plagued many colonists who lived on, or near, the frontier. He visited a Boer family whose house and farm buildings were destroyed about fifteen years earlier by Xhosa fighters, whom he calls 'those ferocious invaders'. The destitute family now lived in what Latrobe described as 'a hovel'. The lady of the house, 'who was a person of better appearance and manners than many of her class', bewailed their situation, asking what was the use of having a decent house and a prosperous farm when they could be attacked at any moment, with their lives and their property always in danger of being destroyed.

A few days later, Latrobe and his party made camp near the banks of the Great Fish River, which was then the boundary between the colony and Caffraria. Although they were not molested, they heard that 'on that very day, the Caffres had stolen fifty head of cattle from the neighbouring farm, and that several boors and soldiers were in pursuit of the thieves'.

Pringle described a catastrophic incident that occurred during one of frontier wars. It led to the abandonment of the Moravian mission station of Enon, which is near to the modern town of Kirkwood, about 100 kilometres inland from Port Elizabeth. The occasion was an attack on herdsmen by Xhosa raiders. Pringle described how the raiders suddenly appeared out of the bush and poured a shower of assegais on to the herdsmen. Only two of the ten men had time to fire their weapons. Although two of the attackers were killed, so were nine of the herdsmen while the tenth escaped with two assegais in his body. The attackers took about 1,000 cattle, which comprised the whole herd of the settlement. Pringle described the men who fell as among the best and most productive in the community and, to add to the loss, all were survived by wives and families. The inhabitants of Enon were not only devastated by the event but, with the theft of the cattle, had lost their main livelihood. They abandoned the settlement and moved to Uitenhage, where they felt safer.

There are at least two parties to any conflict, and dislocations and suffering are usually experienced on all sides. Providing insights into the feelings of those who suffered from the colonial advance, Campbell described an abandoned Xhosa settlement in the Zuurveld and its location as follows:

> we came in sight of a beautiful valley between the mountains of about four miles extent. The sides of the mountains were covered with Caffre gardens among the trees from whence they had lately been driven by the military. The skeletons of many of their houses remained and some tobacco was still growing but the whole of their corn fields were destroyed. The hills were covered with trees to the top and were divided by the course of a river. Formerly the whole was covered with Caffre villages but now there is not a living soul but stillness everywhere reigns… The scenery around was romantic and grand in the highest degree.

It is easy to imagine the resentment and hostility that would be felt by people who had been forced to abandon such a favourable location together with their homes and livelihoods.

In similar vein, Pringle provided an insight into the resentment that must have been felt by Xhosa people who were forced out of their homes when, like Campbell, he described the richness, beauty, and fertility of a part of the Zuurveld from which they were evicted. He wrote,

> The aspect of the country, though wild, was rich and beautiful. It was watered by numerous rivulets, and diversified with lofty mountains and winding vales, with picturesque rocks and shaggy jungles, open upland pastures, and meadows along the river margins, sprinkled as usual with willows and acacias, and occasionally with groves of stately yellow wood… But the remains of Caffer hamlets, scattered through every grassy nook and dell, and now fast crumbling to decay, excited reflections of a very melancholy character…

In his book, Pringle provided several insights into the human costs of conflict and division; in fact, it is likely that these experiences spurred him to take the position of secretary of the Anti-Slavery Society when he returned to Britain in 1827. One incident that Pringle recorded took place in 1820, a few days after he arrived in South Africa, at the mission station of Bethelsdorp where he witnessed a constable leading an African woman who was accompanied by a little girl, as well as by an infant strapped to her back. The woman was one of a group that had crossed the frontier without permission and were now to be given in servitude to some colonists. Pringle described how the woman appealed to the missionary for assistance and railed against her fate:

> Sometimes she raised her tones aloud, and shook her clenched hand, as if she denounced our injustice, and threatened us with the vengeance of her tribe. Then again, she would melt into tears, as if imploring clemency, and mourning for her helpless little ones.

Some of the residents translated her cries for help for the missionary, but he could do nothing except try to console her. Pringle was so affected by the scene that he observed trenchantly that he could not help thinking that his countrymen, who made captives of harmless women and children, 'were in reality greater barbarians than the savage natives of Caffraria'.

Pringle also recorded a conversation with one of his Boer neighbours who described how, when he was a young man and first went on commando, they surprised and destroyed a large settlement of Bushmen. Five women survived the attack and it was decided that they would be apportioned among members of the commando. The captives, who were forced to march in front of the commando, impeded progress because they could not move fast enough, so four of them were shot dead. However, the fifth woman clung to one of the commando members, pleading to be spared. She would not relinquish her grasp and at last the men relented and the man to whom she had clung took her home with him. She served him long and faithfully and, said Pringle's informant, was still doing so, as far as he knew. The man ended his story by saying sombrely, 'May God forgive the land!'

Nevertheless, despite suffering, destruction, traumatic events, reverses and even deaths, the frontier kept expanding. Thompson described the process as follows: a colonist who wanted more land would go beyond the nominal boundary and find a suitable location in Bushman country. Then he would notify the *landdrost* and, at the same time, would forward a memorial to the governor, asking to be awarded the farm. In the meantime, the colonist would continue to occupy the land on which he had settled, which was called a request place until the matter was decided. It is likely that few if any of these memorials were refused because, by approving a request, the authorities in the distant Cape could at least retain a semblance of authority over the roving, independent-minded *trekboers*. Also, it was almost always in the *landdrost*'s nature and interests to support his fellow Boers.

The *trekboers* moved forward and outward for at least two reasons. One reason was that they needed new grazing land because their herds consumed large amounts of grazing and water, and damaged the ecosystem. The second reason was the Boers' desire to establish their children on farms of their own. Thompson referred to this motive when he wrote that the great ambition of the colonists was to see all their children settled upon farms of 6,000 English acres in extent. Campbell was critical of this pattern of existence, because he thought that it was both anti-social and was a 'lazy, wandering, nomadic life'. Philip, ever the (forlorn) champion of the rights of indigenous people, commented on both the family motive, and the view of race and culture, that validated the land seizures when he stated the frontier Boers never thought of dividing their extensive domains among their children, as long as they could find new and suitable land that was unoccupied by colonists. Philip continued by saying that the Boers not only looked upon the Bushmen as an inferior race, but also considered it an injustice that Bushmen should possess anything that a Christian man desired, and so they thought that they had 'the most undisputed right to their fountains'.

Another reason was that the environment became ever more marginal and less supportive of agricultural and pastoral activities as the *trekboers* moved further away from the coast, into arid regions such as Little Namaqualand and the Great Karoo. Lichtenstein described just how precarious was farming in these regions, writing that it was 'one of the evils' of the country that a spring which had yielded a good supply of water since time immemorial would suddenly fail 'and become wholly dried up'. From that moment, said Lichtenstein, all the buildings, gardens, and plantations were as good as lost, and the owner, with all his household, livestock and property, had to look for a new place to settle and begin all over again.

The ongoing expansion of the Colony was accelerated by the fact that many Boers in the frontier areas were so accustomed to the nomadic life that they were fully adapted to living in a wagon. Fisher said that to a *trekboer*, anything that could not be moved from place to place in a wagon was considered superfluous. All that a grazier really needed was a gun, ammunition and a wagon: with these, he could provide himself with almost everything else that he required. The only items that he might purchase were some cotton goods, hats, coffee and sugar. Cloete agreed with this assessment and referred to

> the facility and rapidity with which those migrations took place, and the unconcern with which, even to this day, many of our colonists are ready to flit from one district to another, for the most (apparently) frivolous reasons, taking their chance to find sufficient or better lands in the further wilds of Africa…

Cloete also said of the *trekboers* that their flocks and herds constituted their sole care and delight. Whenever these increased and multiplied, they were content and happy; but when that did not happen, they were ready to move on, to search for lands where recent rains promised grass and water for their cattle.

Henry Cloete, who wrote eloquently about the Great Trek and the Natal Boers, was a descendant of one the first free burghers, and was of mixed Dutch and English ancestry. Although he was born and bred in the Cape, he was educated at the University of Leyden in Holland and then qualified as a lawyer in London. Before he retired as a judge, he was a senior civil servant who undertook important and delicate tasks for the British administration in the Cape. His frustration at the habits of the *trekboers* reflected his perspective as a conscientious civil servant and administrator who was unable to impose order and consistency on the volatile, ever-shifting, independence-loving inhabitants of the frontier.

Adhikari described the situation accurately when he drew attention to 'the weakness of the colonial state and its tenuous control over frontier areas' and noted that this situation 'gave settlers, who had access to arms, wide discretion to act against indigenes'. For more than a century and a half, the frontier was a source of extreme exasperation for the officials at the distant Cape as well as for their representatives in the field, such as *landdrosts* and military officers – and this was true whether the administration was Dutch or British.

Cloete's use of the verb 'flit' to describe the movements of the mobile colonists is hardly appropriate, when one considers the size of a wagon and its team of oxen, as well as the logistical complexities of providing water and sustenance for human beings, oxen and the livestock that accompanied a trekking party. Nevertheless, it expressed Cloete's annoyance at being unable to pin down and control so many of the colonists who were nominally the responsibility of his administration.

For a depiction of wagons flitting across the veld, we can consider Reid's imaginative account of three trekking parties on the move. Reid described

> ...immense vehicles with bodies above four yards in length, surrounded by an arching of bamboo canes covered with canvas. To each is attached eight pairs of long-horned oxen, with a driver seated on the box, who flourishes a whip, in length like a fishing-rod; another on foot alongside, wielding the terrible *jambok*,[6] while at the head of the extended team marches the *foreloper*, *riem* in hand, guiding the oxen along the track. Half a score horsemen ride here and there upon the flanks, with three others in advance; and bringing up the rear is a drove of milch cows – some with

calves at the foot – and a flock of fat-tailed sheep, their tails full fifty pounds in weight, and trailing on the ground.

Although this account is imaginative and dramatic, it does provide an insight into the size of a trekking party, and into the logistics of keeping it moving.

While the *trekboers* did not actually flit, the comparatively rapid pace at which the frontier moved forward on the northern and northeastern fronts can be seen from Philip's report about the Toverberg mission station. Philip wrote that when the Toverberg institution was abolished in 1818, its location was beyond the limits of the colony; however, said Philip, at the time that he was writing, the country around Toverberg was occupied by farmers as far as the Orange River, several days' journey beyond it. Philip's book was published in 1828, so he was probably reflecting the situation a few years earlier in about 1825. To contextualise his remarks, we should know that Toverberg mission was located on the site of the present-day town of Colesberg, which is about twenty-five kilometres south of the Orange River (or Great River). (Incidentally, this was the district in which Paul Kruger spent part of his boyhood.)

Philip was alarmed because within a short period of about eight years the *trekboers*, who had not even reached the site of Toverberg in 1818, had moved as far as the river by the mid-1820s. This would imply that they had advanced the fringe of the colony by about fifty or sixty kilometres within about eight years. Moreover, it appears that Philip was referring to a relatively large number of *trekboers*, because he wrote that the country was peopled with farmers, suggesting that a considerable number had settled in the territory with a view to occupying it permanently. This is also suggested by the fact that Paul Kruger said that he spent some of his boyhood at Vaalbank Farm in the same district; the word 'farm' suggests that the land had been incorporated within the Colony and had been granted to an owner. This can be dated between 1825 (when Kruger was born) and 1835, when the family left the district to trek northwards, although the grant might have been made before 1825. It is also likely that the Kruger clan was among those who settled in the area around the former site of Toverberg and caused Philip such alarm.

Philip was concerned because the region from Toverberg to the Orange/Great River had been permanently settled by *trekboers*; however, this was not the limit of *trekboer* incursions. Cloete stated that the country between the Orange and Vaal Rivers – that is, the territory beyond the Orange River that later became the Orange Free State – was often frequented by *trekboers* because it provided a better supply of grass during the summer months. Nevertheless, although the *trekboers* laid claim to whichever tracts of lands they could find beyond the river, they still returned to their lands within the Colony when the drought ended, or whenever they were called on to pay their annual assessment tax. One of the reasons was that they did not want to lose title and possession of lands that had been granted to them within the Colony.

Theal also noted that *trekboers* moved freely beyond the official border of the Colony and explained that as early as 1819 small parties of European hunters began to penetrate the country between Cornet Spruit and the Caledon, and a few years later they occasionally went as far north as Thaba Bosigo. They only encountered what Theal called a few savage Bushmen and therefore considered that the country was open for them to claim. At about the same time, said Theal,

> some nomadic Boers from the district of Colesberg were tempted to make a temporary residence in the district between the Orange and Modder rivers, on ascertaining that grass was to be found there during seasons of drought in the colony.

As a champion of the rights and welfare of indigenous people, Philip was concerned about Toverberg because the mission stations were the only places in which indigenous people could find refuge, to protect them from being hunted down and/or pressed into service on European farms. This is shown by the fact that about 1,700 Khoi and San (Khoi-San?) people had settled at Toverberg within a short time of its founding in 1814. Only four years later, Toverberg mission station was closed by order of the Governor at the Cape, with no convincing reason given. Philip commented bitterly that the reason was that the country had to be cleared of Bushmen because it was to be allocated to colonists, which could not be done under the eye of a missionary station.

9

The Eastern Frontier

The frontier advanced swiftly in the northern and north-eastern sectors because those regions were relatively arid and thus thinly populated. However, this was not the case on the eastern frontier, where the colonists met the advancing Bantu-speaking tribes, whom the colonists called Kaffirs (also spelled Caffres or Caffers). We have already seen that their advance forced the Gonaqua people to retreat westwards from the Bashee River towards the Fish River, and then progressively further westwards, until they were squeezed between the advancing colonists on the one hand and the advancing Bantu-speakers on the other.

These Bantu-speaking groups (I will call them the Xhosa for convenience, although this is simplistic) were a far more determined and doughty foe than the Khoi and the San. For one thing, they were more numerous; for another, they were better armed and better organised. Proof of the quality of the opposition that Xhosa forces offered is provided by the invasion of the colony that took place in 1818 in retaliation for an attack on Xhosa territory by a combined force of British soldiers and burgher militia. The Xhosa warriors overran the frontier districts, as far as the vicinity of Algoa Bay (Port Elizabeth). Several military posts were captured and small parties and patrols of British troops were cut off. The colonists were driven from the Zuurveld. The mission station of Theopolis, which was close to present-day Port Alfred, was repeatedly attacked, and was only saved by the defence of the Hottentot inhabitants while, as seen, the mission station at Enon was plundered and burned. Farmers in the border areas lost thousands of head of cattle, which were carried off by the raiders. A year later, in 1819, a force of 10,000 Xhosa fighters attacked Grahamstown and almost overran it before being repulsed when reinforcements arrived late in the day. In short, these were not the Khoi and San people, who had been overcome with relative ease; these opponents on the eastern frontier were determined and formidable.

The colonists and the Xhosa-speaking groups first encountered and clashed with each other at some time after the middle of the eighteenth century. For instance, Borcherds wrote that in 1781 'the first commandant in the eastern country' reported that some 'Kaffirs' had occupied land on the western side of the Great Fish River, 'contrary to treaty'. When they ignored instructions to move across to the other side of the river, they were forced to do so, and 5,300 head of cattle, 'partly stolen from the colonists', were captured and divided amongst the men 'who joined the expedition.' The phrase 'contrary to treaty' suggests that there were earlier interactions between the two groups while the phrase 'partly stolen' tells us that, although recovering stolen cattle was often the ostensible cause of war, the commando members usually seized the opportunity to enlarge their herds by theft, if they were victorious.

I will not detail the many frontier wars that took place during the nineteenth century. Suffice to say that although the frontier of the Colony was pushed further eastwards decade by decade, from the Sundays River to the Fish River to the Keiskamma River to the Kei River, it was only after huge efforts were made, involving both regular and irregular troops, and at the cost of ferocious fighting, in which the result often hung in the balance. A piece of territory that was added to the Colony after a war could only be occupied by settlers if they were protected by troops and, even then, they were not always secure. In summary, on the eastern frontier, settlers could not move independently and appropriate land almost at will, as happened on the north-eastern and northern fringes of the Colony.

In fact, the emigrant Boers – that is, those who participated in the

Great Trek – cited frustration with conditions on the frontier as one of the reasons why they left the eastern districts and trekked northwards in a relocation that finally saw many of them settle north of the Vaal River, where they established the Transvaal Republic or ZAR. But more about that later.

Boers only lived predominantly nomadic or semi-nomadic lives on the mobile fringes of the Colony. The more one travelled away from the frontier into districts that had been settled for longer periods of time, the more one encountered solid, spacious, well established homesteads and extensive farming operations. As an insight into one of these, we can attest Pringle's description of the establishment of his party's nearest neighbour, an old Dutch-African Boer, named Wentzel Coetzer. This farm would have been about thirty kilometres north-west of the present-day town of Bedford in the Eastern Cape and thus quite close to the Fish River, which so often formed the eastern boundary of the Colony. While Coetzer's ancestors, and perhaps Coetzer himself, would have been *trekboers* at some time in the past, from Pringle's description of the establishment, the family had been settled there for a considerable period.

Accommodation consisted of 'three or four thatched houses, and a few reed cabins (*hartebeest huisjes*) inhabited by the Hottentot dependants'. Pringle described the main house as being of the size and appearance of an old-fashioned Scottish barn. The walls were thick and were built of strong clay, while the roof was thatched with rushes. Various implements and foodstuffs hung from the rafters: there were weapons of the hunt, dried meat of various kinds of game, large whips, leopard and lion skins, ostrich eggs and feathers, dried fruit, strings of onions, rolls of tobacco, bamboos for whip handles, calabashes, and a variety of other articles. There was a large pile of home-made soap on top of the partition wall.

The house had a main room in the middle, flanked by a bedroom on each side. The windows did not have glass but could be closed with shutters made of zebra skin. Apart from furniture, which was rustic and quite basic, the main room also had two pieces of apparatus for home industry, namely a large butter churn and a large iron pot for boiling soap. The bedrooms had bedsteads with feather mattresses that were spread on frames woven with leather thongs.

Meat was the main item in the family's diet. Pringle was told that two sheep, and sometimes more, were slaughtered every day, to be eaten by the family and their servants. As a sample of the diet, the evening meal, which was the main meal of the day, consisted of mutton broiled and stewed, wheaten bread, butter, milk, and some dishes made of vegetables and dried fruits.

Near to the main building was an orchard with peach, apricot, almond, walnut, apple, pear and plum trees, avenues of figs and pomegranates, and several citrus trees. There was also a kitchen garden in which grew various vegetables. Next to the garden was a vineyard from which the grapes, together with peaches, were mainly used to make brandy. In addition, there were about twenty acres of corn land and a small corn mill.

However, noted Pringle, the real wealth of the farm was in the flocks and herds. There were about 700 head of cattle and about 5,000 sheep and goats. Pringle noted that this was about average for a farmer in that part of the country. When ready for market, stock would be driven all the way to Cape Town, which was about 1,000 kilometres away.

Another indication that this farm had been occupied for a considerable period was the fact that the main cattle pen was raised about five to six metres above the surrounding ground. This was because the pen surmounted a mass of hard, solid dung, which had been deposited over many years.

Thompson's description of a farm in the Sneeuwberge, which is about 200 to 250 kilometres north-north-east of Cape Town and thus much further from the frontier than Coetzer's establishment, described greater degrees of sophistication: there were spoons and other articles of silver, there were 'capacious tureens of well burnished pewter', and plates of China and English delft. The host, who was one of the wealthiest men in the district, had eleven farms pasturing 13,000 sheep and 2,000–3,000 cattle, as well horses and fields of corn.

The Cape Colony was a slave-owning society from the very beginning of the European settlement there. According to Bryce, slaves outnumbered their masters and mistresses when Britain took over the Cape for the second and final time. He estimated that in 1806, the European population of the Colony consisted of about 27,000 persons. There were about 30,000 black slaves, while 'of the aboriginal Hottentots about 17,000 remained'. However, it appears that the frontier Boers had very few slaves in the strict sense of the word, possibly because slaves were expensive, and/or possibly because they were difficult to acquire at such a distance from Cape Town. Rather, as we have seen, the Khoi and San/Bushmen were not only driven away and killed so that the colonists could occupy their land but were also seized and pressed into service in a manner that some observers considered to be worse than slavery. For instance, Pringle observed that the farmers on the frontiers were entirely dependent on the Bushmen for their labour because few, if any, had slaves or Hottentots to do the herding work. That it was a long-standing and approved practice can be seen from Barrow's observations that under the Dutch administration what he termed 'the abominable expeditions which are carried on, under the authority of government' against the indigenous inhabitants were mainly undertaken to capture women and children to work as servants. He noted that the raids by colonists made the indigenous people more savage and revengeful.

The situation did not change much during the first decades of the British administration, which led Philip to accuse his countrymen of hypocrisy. He wrote that 'while England boasts of her humanity, and represents the Dutch as brutes and monsters, for their conduct towards the Hottentots and Bushmen', the conduct of the British administration had been even more oppressive. Philip explicitly referred to the Caledon Code which, as he explained, meant that

Hottentots should be coerced into serving the farmers. Nor did Philip think that the law of 1812 was an improvement, because it required that Khoikhoi children who had been maintained by settlers for their first eight years, could be apprenticed for ten more years. In addition, under these laws, any Hottentots who were not on mission stations had to be in service of either settlers or the state. Philip condemned all these measures outright and wrote trenchantly that the Hottentots' real condition was simply that of slavery. Also, Hottentots who were not resident at a mission station were entirely at the disposal of the local authorities of the district in which they resided. Furthermore, the law made it impossible for indigenous people to own land.

Pringle loyally maintained that these laws improved the situation for the Khoi and San because, although the measures were coercive and restrictive, they did give something with one hand even if they took away with the other hand. What they gave to the affected persons was the necessity of masters providing their labourers with contracts, and the setting out of conditions under which the servants should work and could be punished.

No doubt, there were many reasons why the Caledon Code was promulgated at that time. Primarily, it was a reaction to the anti-slavery movement that was gathering momentum in influential circles in Britain. A law prohibiting slave trading, but not slavery itself, was passed during 1808, thus effectively halting the supply of new slaves in the Empire. Although further progress happened at a snail's pace, it was a prelude to the Slavery Abolition Act of 1833, which applied to almost all British colonies and possessions. With anti-slavery advocacy gaining momentum, the Earl of Caledon had to do something, and to be seen to be doing something, which is undoubtedly the reason for the liberal clauses in the Code. As Cappon notes, at that time there was a strong movement in favour of legislation to protect slaves and indigenous servants in the British colonies from the violence or injustice of their masters.

The restrictive clauses in the code would not only have been concessions to the sensibilities of the farmers, but also a pragmatic recognition that servitude had been happening for many years and that things were not going to change quickly in the short term. Moreover, as always, the authorities in the Cape would have known how difficult it was to enforce an unpopular law in the distant regions of the Colony, especially when local officials, who were usually closely connected with the communities, turned blind eyes to offences.

10

Commandos and 'Bastards'

For the Boers, an essential instrument in raiding and controlling the indigenous inhabitants, and in maintaining supremacy, was the commando system. It was a system that developed on the frontiers of the Colony and that continued to be used in the Transvaal, where there was neither conscription nor a standing army. The commando was an irregular force that was summoned into the field by an officer of the state, usually the *landdrost*, and was commanded by an elected officer such as a field-cornet. A commando consisted of local men who supplied their own arms, horses and basic provisions; eligible men had to be prepared to be called up at any time.

For its effectiveness, a commando relied on several factors. One was its mobility, via the horsemanship and stamina of its members. Another was possession of guns, and the ability to use them effectively. A third was bushcraft, or the ability of the commando members to use the terrain to maximum effect, whether mounted or dismounted. Commando members generally had all these abilities to a high degree, because of their close acquaintance with the land, the many hours that they spent on horseback during their daily lives, and their regular use of guns for hunting.

From Thompson, we have a detailed account of a commando in operation against an enemy force. Although Thompson did not personally witness the encounter, he reported it verbatim from correspondence that he received from missionaries who were eye-witnesses. The missionaries were accompanying Bechuana people[7] who

A battle scene, Voortrekker Monument, Pretoria.

had called on the Griquas to repel an attack from the east. Although the Griquas were of mixed Boer and Khoisan ancestry, and thus not Boers, and although they lived beyond the boundaries of the Colony, they adopted almost all the colonists' technology and methods, and their commando tactics would have been the same as those employed by the Boers. In fact, in the Colony, people of mixed ancestry were often called upon to perform commando services and thus learned the appropriate skills and strategies.

Thompson described an attack by a group called the Mantatees, who were fugitives from the depredations of the Zulu ruler, Chaka. The Mantatees, who were named after their female ruler, were driven westward when Chaka's army attacked tribes that lived to the north and west of the Drakensberg Mountains in the eastern areas of what was later called the Orange Free State. As the Mantatees fled, other fugitives swelled their number. Moving westwards, this large body of people attacked the Bechuana tribes who lived north of the Vaal River, until they were finally checked in the battle that Thompson described.

As already noted, the outward expansion of the *trekboers* placed indigenous people in increasingly marginalised and pressurised situations that caused knock-on effects far beyond the actual areas in which they operated. However, as seen in the case of the Mantatees, other pressures, causing knock-on effects from the opposite direction, were also disrupting many of the tribes in the interior of Southern

Africa. These pressures mainly came from the realignments that were caused by the depredations of the Zulu empire. Groups such as the Xhosa, who lived between the Great Fish River and approximately the area of the southern boundary of the present-day province of Kwa-Zulu Natal, were caught in an ever-closing vice, while other groups, like the Mantatees and the Bapedi (see later) overran weaker groups as they fled westward and northward.

Thompson's correspondent described the Mantatee warriors as follows:

> Their appearance was truly formidable. The warriors were very tall, athletic men, quite black, with no other clothing than a sort of apron round their loins They wore plumes of ostrich feathers on their heads and their weapons consisted of spears or javelins, battle axes, and clubs They had large oval shields which, when rushing forward, they held close to the ground on the left side.

As the forces engaged with each other, the mounted Griquas approached and fired at the Mantatee warriors, and then dismounted. Thompson's missionary correspondent described how the warriors ran swiftly toward the Griquas who, after firing, had to remount their horses hastily and retreat to a safe distance. The battle continued in this fashion for about two hours, with the Griquas alternately advancing and retreating as circumstances dictated. These tactics exhausted and frustrated the Mantatees who, while they were taking many casualties, were unable to get to grips with the Griquas.

Now the Griquas dismounted on higher ground and, with deadly accuracy, began picking off leading figures in the enemy ranks. The correspondent reported that as every shot found a target, the warriors began to show signs of fear and confusion. At this point, the Mantatee's cattle escaped from their herders and the Griquas drove them away. The warriors broke off the engagement and began to move away slowly. True to the commando practice of appropriating as many of the enemy's cattle as possible, the Griquas and their Bechuana allies ended the conflict and drove off as many cattle as they could.

In summary, the commando was an irregular force that was summoned into the field when required. The members provided their own horses, arms and equipment. They were able to fight both on horseback and on foot, they had a good understanding of how to use terrain, and their mobility and excellent marksmanship allowed them to oppose an enemy that was far more numerous. Finally, although they operated as a unit, they did not follow set drills or procedures. Within an overall plan of battle, each man followed his own course of action.

Having mentioned the Griquas, this is an apt place to have another look at the pressures that the advancing colonial frontier exerted on places and people beyond the frontier. On the northern and north-eastern frontiers, one of the main pressures came from groups like the Griquas, who were of mixed Dutch-Khoisan ancestry with an admixture of Tswana blood. Although these mixed ancestry groups were largely European in their customs and habits, they could not live freely and independently within the Colony because of racial prejudice and because they were not accepted as legitimate offspring.

Most of these groups raided neighbouring tribes for livestock and slaves. With their commando-type tactics, they usually prevailed, as the Griquas did in the encounter with the Mantatees. This forced their neighbours further into the interior, where they pressured other tribes, and so on as the ripples moved outwards. For instance, reporting what he heard from a missionary who lived beyond the Colony, Philip described the depredations of a group known as the Bergenaars or Mountain People, whose numbers were swelled by disaffected Griquas and others. Philip wrote that they got ammunition from the Colony and terrorised nearby Bechuana tribes, from whom they stole huge numbers of cattle. Success bred success and their numbers grew as other outcasts joined them. The result, said Philip, was that 'thousands of these wretched people [the Bechuanas] are compelled to wander about in quest of subsistence' and they, in their turn, took to plundering others. From Philip's description, the Bergenaars operated commando-style with horses and rifles; they traded with colonists (probably selling captives as well livestock); and they caused considerable disruption and distress to their neighbours.

Thompson referred to the disruptions caused by the Afrikaner group on the northern frontier, and especially across the Orange River, where they finally settled in what is now Namibia. There they subdued and intermarried with the indigenous Nama people, while setting themselves up as a ruling caste. Thompson stated that in about 1810, 'a bastard Hottentot, named Africaner' collected a band of people of his own race, runaway slaves, and other fugitives and, having got guns and ammunition, plundered the defenceless Namaquas and Korannas. (These were pure Khoi tribes.) He then exchanged the stolen cattle with colonists, for further supplies of arms and ammunition.

In time, the Afrikaners became the most powerful of the Oorlam groups.[8] They dominated most of the central and southern parts of present-day Namibia and by the mid-nineteenth century, from their base in Windhoek, they regularly raided the neighbouring Bantu-speaking Herero clans for cattle.

Incidentally, it is interesting that the first people to use the term Afrikaner to describe themselves, were not whites but people of mixed ancestry. By using this term, they proclaimed that they were people of Africa, in comparison with the Boers, who were prouder of their European heritage. Like most other mixed-ancestry groups, the Afrikaners used Dutch as their high language – that is, the language of literacy, correspondence, religion and external relations – and their descendants in Namibia today are Afrikaans-speaking.

As an example of the position that mixed ancestry groups accorded to Dutch, there is this incident that took place north of the Orange River during the 1840s. At Bethanie, in the south of present-day Namibia, a missionary named Knudsen tried to use the indigenous language, Nama, as the medium of instruction in the mission school. However, the local chief, David Christian, intervened, saying, 'Only Dutch! Nothing but Dutch! I despise myself and want to creep into the bushes for very shame when I speak Hottentot.'

As already seen, mixed-ancestry groups such as the Griquas and Oorlam-Afrikaners arose from sexual relations between male Boers and women of other races, such as female slaves, indentured labourers, or captured Khoi and San women. At one time, the products of these unions were referred to as *Basters* (bastards); however, at some time during the early nineteenth century, the term seems to have fallen out of favour for general use, probably because of its forthrightness. The Boer fathers, and the fathers' families, did not confer legitimacy on the children who were born of these liaisons, probably to keep the Christian race pure and distinctly European. As a result, many of the bastards moved to the peripheries of the Colony. There they banded together with others in similar circumstances, as well as with destitute Khoi and San people, and made their livings by whatever means they could. As seen above, although these mixed ancestry people were rejected by their Boer progenitors, they adopted many aspects of the colonists' habits and technology which gave them ascendancy over the people whom they raided and subjected. They also adopted the colonists' language and religion.

As evidence of how Basters could prosper if given the chance, there is Thompson's description of the establishments of a family named Boukes (probably Beukes). During 1824 or 1825, in the Khamiesberg region, which is about 500 kilometres north of Cape Town, Thompson met a Griqua or Bastard Hottentot named Dirk Boukes who 'seemed more like a substantial boor [Boer] than a destitute Hottentot'. He had large flocks and herds as well as an extensive tract of cultivated land. Thompson wrote that everything was 'on a very respectable footing', except for his house, which was a Namaqua-style hut. Boukes was a member of a large family, and both his father and his brothers had all done equally well for themselves. However, Thompson commented that people like these, being of mixed ancestry, suffered from the great disadvantage of not being able to acquire property in the Colony. The result was that many of them were driven beyond the borders of the Colony where, said Thompson, they were tempted to become outlaws and robbers. If any of them settled on a desirable piece of land, some Boer would drive them away, occupy it, and obtain a grant for the land from the government.

The name Beukes is common among the *Rehoboth Basters* who, in 1868, turned their backs on the Colony and trekked northwards across the Orange River in search of a place that they could call their own, where they could govern themselves under their own *Raad* (council) and constitution. They finally found their place in the *Rehoboth Gebiet* (Rehoboth Territory), which is located about ninety kilometres south of Windhoek in central Namibia. It is possible that the descendants of the Beukes family of the Kamiesberg were among those trekking *Basters* who, having been driven ever further northwards by the advancing fringes of the Colony and being dispossessed all the while, finally shook the dust of the Colony off their feet and moved far beyond its reach.

Dispossession and oppression resulted in a state of lawlessness that spread instability far into the interior. Thompson described some of the disastrous effects by describing how Bechuana clans had been plundered in 'the most unprovoked and cruel manner', while the bandits had dispersed or even destroyed whole tribes by robbing them of their cattle and even their children. The effects, said Thompson, were as bad as the miseries that had been inflicted by the savage Mantatees. He estimated that what he called the Griqua or Bastard population had spread throughout the whole length of the Orange River, over 700 miles, and he estimated that they numbered at least 5,000 people, with at least 700 muskets among them. Thompson expressed his concern at the fact that colonists not only traded for the fruits of the plunder but also, in contravention of the law, sold arms and ammunition to Griqua or Bastard buyers.

By now, it should be clear that Boer society was strongly patriarchal. In fact, only men were included in the ranks of burghers and only they had full civil rights in the two Boer republics. In addition, in this society as in similar ones elsewhere, while patriarchal males used their dominant positions to have sexual relations with subordinate females, they only recognised the offspring of their legitimate unions as members of their families and as heirs. As we have seen, this largely accounted for the large number of outcast and property-less people of mixed ancestry in the Colony, as well as for the many outcasts who operated on its fringes. It also accounts for the fact that many members of these groups had typical Boer names and for the fact that although they were usually bi- or multilingual, they had Dutch (later Afrikaans) as their high language.

11

Dissatisfaction

As we have seen, on the eastern frontier the colonists often found themselves on the back foot in the face of Xhosa incursions that destroyed property, took lives, forced colonists to flee, and captured their livestock. Historians give the name Frontier Wars to the most significant of these clashes, and it is the one that is called The Sixth Frontier War that had the most profound impact on the group of people that became known as the Transvaal Boers.

By 1834, the British administration at the Cape had pushed the colonial frontier as far eastwards as the Keiskamma River and had expelled the Xhosa from the region between the Fish and Keiskamma Rivers. This region, which was called the Ceded Territory, was settled by colonists[9] and loyal Bantu-speaking groups. The Xhosa groups were now facing severe pressures as their territory contracted in the west because of the advance of the colonial frontier, and in the east because of the expansion of the Zulu empire. Inevitably, the Xhosa people's impoverishment and declining resources led to numerous raids on the colonists' cattle. Matters came to a head when an attack by a government-authorised commando incensed the Xhosa and in retaliation, an army of ten thousand men swept across parts of the Colony, pillaging and burning homesteads and forcing refugees from farms and villages to take refuge in Grahamstown.

To oppose the Xhosa forces, Boer commandos and settler irregulars mobilised and the authorities brought in Imperial troops. By the time the conflict ended during September 1836, the casualties and damages on the colonists' side included forty dead farmers and 416 farmhouses burned, as well as the loss of 5,700 horses, 115,000 head of cattle and 162,000 sheep that had been plundered by the invaders. In retaliation, as usual, Xhosa cattle were taken or retaken by the colonists. The Xhosa would also have suffered considerably from losses in life and property.

This conflict was the catalyst for the mass emigration that is known as the Great Trek, which took place during the late 1830s and early 1840s. During these years, thousands of Boer families, accompanied by servants and other dependants, left the eastern districts of the Colony and trekked northwards. While there is some disagreement about the full and exact reasons for the trek, there is no doubt that the trekkers wanted to escape from British rule and settle in places where they could govern themselves.

One of the best known of the trekkers, Piet Retief, drafted a manifesto in which he explained the emigrant's motives and their hopes for their new lives. He gave the following as their main reasons for leaving the Colony:

> The country was beset with 'the turbulent and dishonest conduct of vagrants, who are allowed to infest the country in every part.'
> They had sustained severe losses because of the emancipation of their slaves.
> They suffered from 'a continual system of plunder…from the Kaffirs and other coloured classes…which has desolated the frontier districts, and ruined most of the inhabitants.'
> An unjustifiable odium had been cast upon them by persons who operated under the cloak of religion; this testimony was believed in Britain and would ruin the country.

Further, Retief stated that although they would not allow slavery when they settled elsewhere, they would 'maintain such regulations as may suppress crime and preserve proper relations between master and servant'. He also stated that they intended to live 'in peace and friendly intercourse' with any native tribes that they encountered.

Cloete wrote that Piet Retief suffered severe losses after war broke out in 1834 and that, when the authorities allowed the 'Kafirs' to have free passage into the Colony after the end of the war, he despaired of having security for his life and property in future. These would have been the experiences and feelings of many Boers, who would have suffered severe losses, both in lives and property, and then would have felt that they were neither recompensed nor protected from suffering further losses.

One writer, Cappon, was convinced that the issue of expansion of territory was a major reason for the trek. He wrote that the Boers strongly believed that, both as white men and as Christians, they had superior rights to dispossess their heathen neighbours. Because they believed that they could expand their territory whenever and wherever they wished, they were in constant conflict with the government; and this, in Cappon's view, was one of the main causes for the trek. On the other hand, reviewing the matter some years after the event – after having lived through it – Cloete declared that the three great causes that underlay the Great Trek were: 1. the Hottentot question; 2. the slave question; and 3. the Kaffir question.

The Hottentot question mainly referred to Ordinance 50 of 1828, which gave Coloureds a degree of equality with the white population. Ordinance 50 repealed the Caledon Code of 1809, which, as stated above, required all Khoi in the Cape to have a fixed place of abode and stipulated that Khoi servants could only leave their place of employment if they carried a pass signed by their employers. Further, in terms of Ordinance 50, Hottentots and other free persons of Colour would have the right to own land and were no longer required to enter contracts as indentured labourers; in fact, the Ordinance required employers to provide service contracts to their employees.

The slave question referred to the fact that in 1833 the British Parliament passed the Slavery Abolition Bill to end slavery in the British Empire. In terms of the act, slaves were apprenticed to their masters for a further period of four years to enable the slaves to learn trades and to allow a transition period for the owners, after which the slaves were to be set free. A sum of money was granted as compensation, which the owners had to collect personally in Britain. This caused dissatisfaction in the colonies, where many people not only regarded the compensation as inadequate, but also complained that it hardly covered the costs involved in travelling to Britain to claim the money. Of course, there was also the matter of the inconvenience and disruption of being away from home for a long time.

Although Retief's manifesto included the slave issue as a major grievance, it has often been pointed out that most people who actually joined the trek, namely the Boers on the eastern frontier, had very few slaves. Rather, it is likely that Retief was expressing an objection to the fact that ex-slaves had joined bands of homeless Hottentots in roaming about the Colony, thus arousing feelings of resentment and insecurity in the colonists. In addition, Retief probably included the issue to broaden the manifesto to cover the grievances of slave-owning Boers in other parts of the Colony.

The 'Kaffir' question referred to a matter that is mentioned in Retief's Manifesto, namely that 'a continual system of plunder… from the Kaffirs and other coloured classes…has desolated the frontier districts, and ruined most of the inhabitants'. The injuries and damages suffered during the 1834–36 frontier war would have been fresh in people's minds at the time that Retief wrote his manifesto. Other issues that caused resentment were the facts that the authorities vacillated in their policies on frontier matters; for instance, after the frontier was advanced to the Kei River, a distance of about 300 kilometres (depending on where it is measured), within a short space of time it was retracted to the Keiskamma River. The Boers also complained that the British government accused Boers of having provoked the most recent war, by their aggressive retaliations for cattle raids.

Retief's manifesto referred to 'an unjustifiable odium' that had been cast upon the Boers by persons who operated under the cloak of religion. He was referring to missionaries who had made known their views that the indigenous inhabitants of the Cape Colony had been harshly treated, and who had advocated equal treatment for all inhabitants of the Colony. The colonists' bête noire was John Philip who, having earlier toured the Cape and published his opinion that colonists treated coloured persons badly, was appointed superintendent of the London Missionary Society's stations in South Africa. It was a time when agitation for the abolition of slavery was gaining strength, and Philip's charges against the colonists and the colonial government found powerful support. Cappon summed up Philip's ideas and effect by saying that he advocated legal equality as far as possible between the white and the coloured races. Philip also held that it was impossible to educate or civilise the native races if they were kept under legal disabilities which degraded them and left them at the mercy of Boer magistrates. Cappon noted that although Philip's views were like those of many missionaries, 'his superior ability and energy in advocating them' made the work of the London Missionary Society especially effective. Obviously, Philip and some missionaries, on the one hand, and the majority of colonists, including most Boers, on the other hand, would be implacably opposed to each other.

In 1823, Philip went back to England to lobby for the rights of indigenous and coloured people. Philip's unpopularity in South Africa grew when his recommendations were adopted by the House of Commons. It was largely owing to Philip that the British government instructed the Cape government to pass the ordinance of 1828, by which free coloured persons at the Cape were granted the same rights as any other British subjects. In the same year, Philip's book *Researches in South Africa* was published; predictably, it did not improve his popularity with the colonists.

To compound his offences in the eyes of the colonists, in 1836 Philip returned to England in the company of two converted Christians, a Coloured and a Xhosa, as well as two fellow missionaries. They gave evidence before a parliamentary committee and aroused public opinion against the Cape government that led to the governor being replaced. Then, piling offence upon offence, Philip returned to the Cape as unofficial adviser to the government on all matters affecting the indigenous people of Southern Africa.

A generation before Philip, another bête noire of the colonists was Johannes van der Kemp (or Vanderkemp), a missionary of the London Missionary Society. After a chequered early life, in 1803 he established a mission settlement for vagrant Hottentots at Bethelsdorp near present-day Port Elizabeth. Local farmers, who were deprived of their free labor by this move, accused Van der Kemp of harbouring lawless elements. He countered with a list of alleged offences against the Hottentots by local farmers, but the evidence proved unsatisfactory and the farmers were acquitted. Nevertheless, the battle lines had been drawn. Van der Kemp further antagonised the colonists when he married a freed slave who was forty-five years his junior and had four children with her, while his missionary colleague, James Read, married a Khoi woman. In doing so, both violated the colour bar that the European settlers had erected to protect their hegemony: as we have seen, although the colonists freely engaged in sexual relations across the colour spectrum, the progeny were social outcasts in colonial society. Legalising an inter-racial relationship, particularly within the sanctity of the church, was a social aberration, if not blasphemous, in the opinions of the colonists. Furthermore, at Bethelsdorp the missionaries not only made converts but also taught literacy, thus challenging the colonists' dictums that all indigenous people were both irredeemably savage and incapable of becoming Christians.

To compound the opprobrium with which Van der Kemp was regarded by the colonists, he pioneered the study of the Xhosa and Khoikhoi languages, thus giving them a scientific and academic status that implied that they were not barbarous and unsystematic. In fact, Van der Kemp aroused such great opposition that the governor ordered him to leave Bethelsdorp for a time.

Cloete referred to the aversion that many of the colonists had for some of the missionaries when he stated that the charges that were brought by Van der Kemp and read against members of influential families, caused hatred toward those missionaries and distrust of the government, from the manner in which the authorities appeared to give credence to the accusations. Reitz, in his apologia for the Boer position that was published just before the war of 1899–1902, had the same opinion and complained that missionaries of the London Missionary Society slandered the Boers, and accused them of inhuman cruelties to the natives. He further complained that these libellous stories were widely believed in Britain, with the result that the Boers were persecuted.

Moodie expressed a view that would have been shared by many of his British fellow colonists when he wrote that although the missionaries would probably not deliberately urge the slaves to rebel, their ignorant fanaticism might well have that result. He continued by dismissing the missionaries as people who came from the lowest class of society and were therefore ignorant about human nature. In fact, he wrote, they were only acquainted with religious dogma, which was warped and perverted from the original simplicity of the faith. In other words, in this view, the missionaries were well-intentioned but naïve, with no understanding of the likely effects of their efforts. It was an opinion that would have been shared by many colonists, both Boer and British.

The enmity between the settlers and many of the missionaries arose from, and reflected, the different influences to which the two groups had been exposed. The Boers, especially those on and near the frontier, had no formal education and little interest in the great movements and ideas, both political and philosophical, which swept over Europe during the seventeenth and eighteenth centuries. In fact, in both a literal and a metaphorical sense, the *trekboers* had been trekking away from them for more than a century. On the other hand, the missionaries were fresh out of Europe and had been imbued with Enlightenment ideas as well as with the spiritual fervour that characterised many of the influential supporters of radical causes. For instance, Cappon referred to the support that Philip's book, 'which exposed the wrongs of the

Hottentots, regarded as human beings', had in Britain, where 'Fowell Buxton, Brougham, Macintosh took up the question, and proposed to raise it in the House of Commons'. He regarded Philip and his supporters as prime movers of the laws that affronted many of the settlers, when he wrote disapprovingly that the result was the repeal of the vagrancy and apprenticeship laws, and the granting of equal rights to non-white people.

Buxton, Brougham and Macintosh were all leading lights in the anti-slavery movement. They, together with other prominent radicals such as William Wilberforce, would have been regarded as anathema by most of the Boers, by many of the newly arrived British settlers, and by many of the governors and administrators. In fact, the Enlightenment, with its radical ideas, its writers, its thinkers, and its activists, stopped a long way short of Cape Town, except in the minds and libraries of a few, isolated individuals (mainly missionaries) who, when they reached the interior and tried to act on those ideas, were faced with baffled obduracy and outright resistance. As Lichtenstein put it, the colonists 'live entirely among themselves, and have therefore no opportunities of gaining any enlarged stock of ideas'.

Earlier, I referred to Cappon's assertion that the issue of expansion of territory was one of the chief causes of the trek. There are good reasons for thinking that Cappon is correct in giving the issue such prominence. Firstly, the number of colonists on the eastern frontier was expanding rapidly, not only because of natural increase, but also through the addition of about four thousand British settlers in 1820. Secondly, the uncertain situation on the frontier, the vacillating policies of the authorities, and the resolute opposition of the Xhosa clans, made it difficult to acquire and securely hold land anywhere east of the Fish River: and it was those regions that were the most fertile and hence the most desirable. This being the case, the would-be trekkers would have been greatly encouraged when a reconnaissance party reported that the land of Natal was not only fertile but was almost empty of inhabitants. They could circumvent the Xhosa tribes by trekking northwards through what became the Orange Free State, and then could turn southwards into Natal. Of course, as later events showed, there were two great drawbacks, namely that the route was guarded by Moselikatse, while the destination was guarded by Dingane, king of the Zulus, who did not want settlers in the region.

Finally, it is worth bearing in mind Cappon's statement that 'ninety-eight per cent of the Boers who made the great trek, from 1836 to 1839, came from the old district of Graaff-Reinet alone'. This, said Cappon, proved that the troubles that caused the trek were all to be found in the frontier district. It focuses attention on the fact that while factors such as the abolition of slavery and the accusations of the missionaries annoyed many Boers in every part of the Colony, all the way from Cape Town to the furthest frontiers, the irritants were not sufficiently annoying to get the whole population moving. Specific events on the eastern frontier tipped the scale there, to motivate thousands of people to join the mass migration: among those events would have been the losses suffered during the latest war, anger at inadequate compensation, the strong suspicion that they would see it all again, and frustration at being checked in their desire to expand into new territories. These would have been amongst the key events and sentiments that were the tipping points on the eastern frontier.

12

The Great Trek

The history of the Great Trek has been covered by many writers and from many angles, so I will only go over it in broad detail. It was an epic event, and it speaks volumes for the determination and motivations of the Boers who were involved that they were prepared to abandon their homes and property and set off for parts unknown. Although it might not have been so disruptive for the *trekboere*, who were semi-nomadic in any case, for the settled *grensboere* (literally frontier farmers), it meant abandoning houses, gardens, orchards, plantations and kraals. I do not know whether Thomas Pringle's neighbours, Wentzel Coetzer and his family, left their property with its large house, orchard, garden and fields, to join the trek. However, whether they did or not, there would have been many farming families with just such large, well developed, and prosperous establishments who did abandon their homes and livelihoods to join the growing lines of wagons that rolled northward across the Orange River, and from there into parts almost unknown.

Backhouse alluded to a little-mentioned aspect of the possessions and property that many of the trek-joining Boers left behind when he wrote that, despite the difficulties and dangers of life in Natal, one of the colonial newspapers continued to publish reports that suggested that there were no dangers in the hinterland. The reason, said Backhouse, was that some of the British settlers were 'planting' letters and reports in the newspaper to encourage Boers to join the trek so that non-trekking colonists could acquire their property and possessions cheaply.

In later years, the trek became the defining event in Afrikaner

The Karel Landman monument near Alexandria, Eastern Cape, South Africa – erected after 1938 to memorialise a Great Trek party.

history and mythology. Perhaps this is ironic because, in fact, only a minority of Boers were involved, and they were almost all from only one region of the Colony and therefore from only one part of Boer society. The fact is that the great majority of Boers stayed home and did not join the trek. Nevertheless, in later years the trek came to represent what were celebrated as essential Afrikaner qualities such as hardihood, love of independence, self-reliance, mutual support, piety and faith in the Almighty, and devotion to the *volk*. Also, it came to exemplify Afrikaner destiny: because, surely, the Almighty had guided His people safely through so many hazards and perils until, finally, they arrived in the Promised Land, where they could settle down and govern themselves, a people apart, according to their own ways?

In this iconic event, two incidents stand head and shoulders above all the others in their contributions to the mythology.

The first was the defeat of Moselikatse, and the second was the Battle of Blood River. Moselikatse was a renegade Zulu captain who, in fleeing from the wrath of Chaka, established his own realm and reign of terror in parts of the territories that became the Transvaal and the Orange Free State. The trekkers first made acquaintance with his followers, the Matabele, when several isolated and unprepared trekker encampments were attacked, causing severe loss of life and property. In his *Memoirs*, Paul Kruger recounts the sequel to those attacks:

> After this massacre the Matabele went back to their town, taking the cattle with them; but they returned a fortnight later in great numbers and attacked the emigrants at Vechtkop [Vegkop], in the Orange Free State. But here Sarel Celliers had built a strong laager (a defensive circle of wagons) and, with the eighty-eight men whom he had at his disposal, repelled the impetuous attacks of the Zulus from his wagon fortress, causing them heavy losses.

The battle also became a significant incident in Boer mythology, as evidence that the Boers, by their own combined efforts together with assistance from Providence, had been delivered from the deadly threat of overwhelming and hostile forces.

Later, in a series of engagements, Boer commandos, with young Paul Kruger in their ranks, forced Moselikatse and his followers to flee as far as the western areas of modern Zimbabwe, which are still called Matabeleland. There the Matabele established a kingdom that was destroyed by the forces of Cecil Rhodes's British South Africa Company during the 1890s.

In passing, it can be noted that the Matabele were probably completely unprepared for the destructive power of the musket volleys that mowed down the warriors. Nor would the Matabele have known how effective a Boer commando was. Until 1829, when the missionary, Robert Moffatt, visited him, Moselikatse was so unacquainted with European technology and methods that he had never seen a wagon; and the Battle of Vegkop took place only seven years later, in 1836.

The other and major stand-out event in Boer mythology is the Battle of Blood River, which took place on 16 December 1838. The lead-up to this event was the movement of many trekboers into the north-western regions of what is today the province of Kwa-Zulu Natal, where they intended to establish an independent republic. To do this, they needed the agreement of the powerful and despotic

Dingane, king of the Zulus. Dingane parleyed with the Boer leader, Piet Retief, and signed an agreement that allowed the Boers to establish their republic. However, Dingane did not want to have Boers as neighbours, and he ordered Retief and all his companions to be killed on the day on which they were to start their return journey, bearing the charter. Subsequently, Dingane's warriors attacked unsuspecting Boer parties and killed more than 500 men, women and children before the remaining Boers, now forewarned, managed to form laagers and fight off the attacking impis.

The Boers in Natal called for reinforcements and assistance from their fellows in the regions that became known as the Transvaal and the Orange Free State, as well as from the frontier regions of the Cape Colony. Thus fortified, a punitive expedition of about 500 men and sixty wagons set out to defeat Dingane. They were aided by the fact that loyalties in the Zulu kingdom were divided, with several of Dingane's brothers having aspirations to the throne.

By this time, two years after Vegkop, the wagon laager had been completely incorporated into the trekkers' military tactics. In fact, their march towards Dingane's heartland seems to have been the first time that the trekkers used a laager as an element in their attacking strategy and not only as a defensive measure. After every day's progress, as the expedition drew ever nearer to its goal, the expedition set up a laager. Finally, at the site that is now known as Blood River, they set up a laager and waited for the attack. It came in the form of about 30 000 Zulu warriors – although the exact number is disputed – and the result was that about 3,000 warriors were killed, while the Boers had only three men lightly wounded.

This defeat severely dented Dingane's reputation and effectiveness. Soon afterwards, his brother, Mpande, who was aligned with the trekkers, defeated Dingane in battle and took over the throne. He granted the trekkers a large stretch of land, where they established the Republic of Natalia, with the newly founded settlement of Pietermaritzburg as its capital. One of the first buildings that was constructed was the Church of the Vow, which commemorated the vow that the commando members were reputed to have repeated every evening during the period that they were moving towards the final battle with Dingane's forces.

This is the vow that came to have such a central place in Afrikaner mythology:

> My brothers and fellow citizens, here we stand in the presence of the Holy God, creator of heaven and earth, to make a vow unto Him, that if His protection shall be with us and He give our enemy into our hand so that we might be victorious over him, that this day and date every year shall be spent as a memorial and a day of thanksgiving, just as a Sabbath is spent and that we shall erect a temple to His honour wherever it will be pleasing to Him and that we shall also instruct our children that they must also share in it, as well as for our generations yet to come. Because the Honour of His name shall thereby be glorified, and the glory and honour of the victory shall be given Him.

During the early twentieth century, the vow and the victory that followed became centrepieces in the mythology of Afrikaner trajectory and destiny, which took its liturgy and its example from the liberation from bondage of the Children of Israel, as they were led to the Promised Land by divine guidance and protection. Of course, in constructs such as divine intervention delivering enemies into the hands of the Chosen People, observing a day of thanksgiving, and erecting a temple, the vow itself is replete with analogies to the Children of Israel and their search for the Promised Land.

However, the Republic of Natalia was not to be the Promised Land. After a military stand-off and convoluted political moves, Natal became a British colony during 1843. In response, most of the Boers once again turned their backs on the hated British and trekked northwards over the Drakensberg Mountains, backtracking on their earlier routes. Once more, they were searching for a place where they could establish their own republic, free of foreign interference.

The retreating Boers would have been angry, saddened, and

frustrated. They had lost hundreds of lives in clashes with the Matabele and the Zulus, they had lost enormous numbers of livestock (although some of those losses were recovered after their victories), they had lost possessions and equipment, they had endured suffering and hardship, and now they had lost the territory that they had won by force of arms and political stratagem. The fact that their republic had been snatched from them after they had done the hard work of securing it, would have caused them to harbour even deeper resentment towards the British. In fact, as Reitz records, in repudiating the annexation of Natal as a British colony, the *Volksraad* (literally people's council or parliament) at Pietermaritzburg addressed the following words of bitter defiance to the British authorities:

> We know that there is a God, who is the Ruler of heaven and earth…and everything we possess, we will with due submission acknowledge to have deserved from Him, but not from men. We are aware of the power of Great Britain, and it is not our object to defy that power; but at the same time, we cannot allow that might instead of right shall triumph, without having employed all our means to oppose it.

In other words, it was the view of the members of the *Volksraad* that although Britain was able to annex Natal because of military might, the annexation was a gross injustice against their people.

The loss of Natalia also foiled the Boers' plans to secure an outlet to the sea that was free of British control. Now, forced back into the interior, they would have to start planning anew.

However, the trekkers would not have taken only frustrations, suspicions, and disappointments with them as they trekked back over the Drakensberg Mountains and into the interior. They must have had a heightened confidence in their ability to prevail over enemies by force of arms, an enhanced sense of community, a belief that they could be masters of their own destinies, a determination not to trust anyone else with, or share with anyone else, their territory and decision-making, and a growing belief that they were special children of Providence.

During the short period of the existence of the Republic of Natalia, the Boers set up the basic pillars of a state. Its structures embodied the ideals that they had fostered for so long, which were given their first expression in the proclamation of a republic in rebellious Graaff-Reinet in 1799. Cloete described the political structure of Natalia as follows: The country was divided into twelve wards. Annually, the inhabitants of each ward chose two persons as their representatives for the ensuing year. These formed a *Volksraad* of twenty-four members, in which were vested executive, legislative, and judicial powers. The *Volksraad* met at Pietermaritzburg on a quarterly basis, and at each meeting a new chairman was chosen from among the members present. All the members performed their duties free of charge; however, to administer the business of government, *landdrosts* with judicial authority were appointed at Pietermaritzburg, Durban and Weenen. Because of the distances involved and the difficulties of travel, an executive committee sat at Pietermaritzburg, to handle urgent business.

Although Cloete had a Boer background (but British sympathies) and was able to understand and represent the grievances of the Boers, his sympathies were neither democratic nor republican. His opinion of the arrangements for governing the Republic of Natalia was that the Boers were heading for a state of anarchy because they lacked a head to direct them or a power to control them. Consequently, they would be entirely guided by instincts. Cloete clearly believed that society is properly ordered when it has a hierarchical structure; according to this view, the mass of humanity requires guidance and leadership from those who, by birth and custom, are best able to perform these functions. This is an elitist or hierarchical view of government and social organisation that views the alternative, which can be called the democratic will or democratic freedom of expression, as inevitably resulting in chaos.

In fact, Cloete claimed that his views were vindicated by the actual events. According to him, the *landdrost* of Pietermaritzburg 'was so constantly thwarted by the ignorant and busy intermeddling of the

Committee Council (*Commissie Raad*) that he soon resigned the office, and no entreaties or prayers could induce him to resume it'. Further, Cloete deplored the fact that decisions of the council were viciously criticised by political opponents. Then, to compound the offence, after some members of the 'opposition' had indulged in 'the most outrageous personal attacks', they were again assailed by 'the reproaches and taunts of the selfish and the interested'.

Shorn of Cloete's disapproving hyperbole, the dissents and disagreements that he describes seem to be normal in democracies, especially if it is remembered that the state of Natalia had been established only recently by people who, whatever their ideals, had no practical experience of self-government. Nevertheless, for good or for ill, it was a model that the Boers would take with them to the Transvaal and the Orange Free State – with these exceptions, that as those states became more complex, they appointed presidents who served for fixed terms, and established administrative structures to provide stability and continuity.

Somewhere along the way, during the seventeenth and early eighteenth century, the Boers had not only cultivated a desire for representative democracy but had also devised a model that turned out to be both simple and effective. This is noteworthy for at least two reasons. Firstly, they had few if any examples to follow because at that time, most states were hierarchical and unrepresentative. However, there were two dispensations that were both republican and representative: one was the United States of America, and one was the convention that came out of the French Revolution, in which all males of twenty-five years of age and above were eligible to vote.

Natalia was one of the earliest states in the modern era to institute universal male suffrage. The timing makes it more unexpected and perhaps even paradoxical that this most conservative of societies – patriarchal, racist, colonial, isolationist and religiously fundamentalist – should have developed and adopted a system of government that was so radical for its time.

Of course, it should be remembered that 'universal male' only meant all males who were accepted as members of the body politic: namely white men who were members of the Dutch Reformed Church (and, later, of sister churches of the Calvinist family).

Although there do not seem to be any records of deliberations and negotiations that led to the adoption of such a radical model of government, it is obvious that the system did not spring forth fully formed, as it were. The model must have developed out of numerous discussions at places where Boers got together, including around the camp fires while on trek. Also, it is very likely that the events of the French Revolution, distilled to their essentials by distance and isolation, provided an inspiration for the structures of a future Boer state. As in France, it would be republican, and it would be representative. In fact, Lichtenstein, who visited Graaff-Reinet and other frontier districts about a decade after the first rebellion there, alluded to the influence of the French Revolution when he wrote that one of the colonists whom he met there, had not taken part in the disturbances, but 'was a zealous advocate for freedom and the natural rights of man'. He knew about all the great public events in Europe during the last fifteen years, and so much admired some of the leading heroes of the French Revolution, that one of his sons was called John Bonaparte, and the other Nicholas Moreau. Later, Lichtenstein recorded that when some colonists were trying to discredit an official, they claimed that at the time of the disturbances in Graaff Reinet, he had worn a symbol of the French Revolution, namely the tricoloured cockade.

On the other hand, the influence of the French Revolution should not be overstated. In the first place, republicanism and the principles and practices of basic democratic governance, as at the congregational level, were generated by the Boers' strong Calvinism. European revolutionary ideas and events would probably only have fortified existing ideas and practices.

As I said earlier, Cloete depicted the governmental structures and practices of Natalia as recipes for the chaos that did, in fact, occur in his view. However, any chaos that ensued, in the form of quarrelling, repudiations and divisive disagreements, was probably mainly attributable to the intense individuality that characterised the Boers, to the birth pangs of a new state, and to the fluidity of their associations while on trek, rather than to the system of government. It should be remembered that these were frontier people who had not only spent most of their lives at the outer limits of central authority but had often actively tried to avoid the reach and demands of authority. They did not easily accept external regulation. In a nutshell, at this point in their history, these Boers were very good at banding together for mutual defence but were less inclined to relinquish some of their rights to centralised authority, even if it was of their own making.

Another feature of the state that the Boers established in Natal was that it was small, even tiny, in terms of the number of citizens. In addition, it was culturally and linguistically homogenous. These features, together with its embryonic nature, probably go a long way to explaining why it did not have a clear separation among the three branches of the state, namely the legislature, the executive, and the judiciary. As we will see, this lack of separation of functions was a feature of the Boer state in the Transvaal, and even had reverberations when Afrikanerdom gained political power over South Africa as a whole.

13

The Transvaal

Although Paul Kruger does not seem to have been present at the battle of Vegkop, and certainly was not present at the battle of Blood River, he was a member of one of the commandos that drove the Matabele forces out of the territory that became the Transvaal. Following the defeat of the Matabele, the Kruger party first settled at a site south of the Vaal River and then crossed the river to settle around present-day Potchefstroom during 1840. Kruger said, 'At last the wanderers had found a comparatively safe home.' By this, he meant that there was little possibility of attacks by enemies, because the Matabele had fled far to the north where they, in turn, had either wiped out or incorporated any tribes that stood in their way.

At first, the Boers settled in the southern regions of what came to be called the Transvaal. The area that they occupied extended from the Vaal River to the Magaliesberg Mountains, which run in an east-west direction north of the present-day city of Pretoria. This region is part of the Highveld, which also includes most of the Free State as well as adjacent regions. The Highveld lies at altitudes between 1,500 and 2,000 metres, and mainly consists of rolling, grassy plains with some rocky ridges. As stated, once the Matabeles had been driven away, it appears that the Boers experienced no further opposition to their settling there.

North of the Highveld is the extensive region known as the Bushveld, which stretches beyond the Magaliesberg Mountains. This largely subtropical region is generally covered with grasslands and bush;

although it is suitable for grazing, few of its regions support agriculture. Large parts of the Bushveld had not been occupied by the Matabele and therefore were not devoid of inhabitants when the Boers expanded their reach into parts of the region. This led to numerous clashes.

Although the trekkers thought that they were freeing themselves of British authority when they trekked away from the Colony, the British authorities thought otherwise. In their view, the trekkers remained British subjects and were subject to British authority, no matter where they were. The first concrete manifestation of this point of view was when Natal, including the Boer republic of Natalia, was annexed as a British colony. As we have seen, many Boers turned away in disgust and trekked back over the Drakensberg Mountains into the interior.

However, British authority followed them. In 1848 the governor at the Cape, Sir Harry Smith, proclaimed the area between the Orange and the Vaal Rivers to be British territory under the name of Orange River Sovereignty. Once more, as happened in Natal, thousands of disgusted Boers moved northwards to join their fellows on the other side of the Vaal River, where they were free of British authority.

The Orange River Sovereignty was a strange and muddled little episode in South African history. The British authorities at the Cape thought that it was a good idea, while their superiors in London were less enthusiastic about it. However, despite the doubts in London, on 3 February 1848, the impulsive Governor, Sir Harry Smith, proclaimed

Crossing the Drakensberg Mountains – mythologising the Great Trek, from a panel in the Voortrekker Monument.

the Sovereignty. A nominated legislative council was created, a high court was established, negotiations with Moshesh and other chiefs fixed the boundaries, and other steps were taken for the orderly government of the country.

Many of the Boers in the territory resented the annexation and soon Andries Pretorius, the hero of Blood River, led a commando southward from the Transvaal to evict the British from the Sovereignty. With a small army of regular troops, Sir Harry Smith confronted the commando at Boomplaats (near Bloemfontein) and, after a short, indecisive battle, Pretorius withdrew his men.

Although the withdrawal meant that the British were nominally in control of the territory, their authority was never secure. One of the main problems was that the British Resident did not have sufficient force to maintain his authority. There were ongoing hostilities between Moshesh, the neighbouring clans, and the European settlers, while there was always the threat of a rebellion by local Boers, supported by their compatriots across the Vaal River.

The British government, which had reluctantly agreed to the annexation of the country, later revised its decision, even although most of the whites in the Sovereignty favoured British rule. At that time, there were about 15,000 white settlers in the territory, of which many were of British background. Boer opposition to the annexation was muted because many of the Boers who were most opposed to British rule had left the Sovereignty and trekked northwards across the Vaal River.

In 1854, the British representative came to an agreement with members of the republican party in the territory and, following the signing of the Orange River Convention, the independent republic of the Orange Free State came into being. Now Britain had recognised two independent Boer republics, because two years earlier, in the face of a renewed threat of an invasion from the north led by Andries Pretorius, the British and the Emigrant Boers north of the Vaal signed the Sand River Convention. This was a red-letter occasion for the emigrants because in terms of the convention, Britain formally recognised the independence of the Boers north of the Vaal River and granted them the right to govern themselves, according to their own laws, free from British interference. Other clauses stated that Britain would not seek alliances with coloured persons north of the Vaal River; that there would be no slavery; and that the arms trade would be strictly controlled, with neither arms nor munitions sold to natives. The convention also included clauses that dealt with extradition, recognition of marriages, and the right of free movement.

Although Kruger reported the event in a matter-of-fact manner, the Boers north of the Vaal River would have regarded the convention as a pivotal moment in their strivings for a place of their own that was independent, republican, self-governing and clearly demarcated. The signing of the convention must have been received with both relief and jubilation.

Ironically, instead of calming passions, the withdrawal of British authority and the creation of an independent Orange Free State exacerbated tensions amongst the various Boer groups so much that it nearly led to civil war. In his memoirs, Kruger explained that the British officials who were arranging the hand-over invited Andries Pretorius to assume authority in the Orange Free State. However, he died before the invitation reached him and his son, Marthinus Wessel Pretorius, who had been appointed commandant general in his father's stead, claimed that the invitation now applied to him. Accordingly, he raised a commando, which was confronted at the Vaal River by a group of Boers who had already formed a government in the Orange Free State. To complicate matters, the Free Staters had summoned the help of a group of Boers from the northern areas of the Transvaal, which had not yet joined the South African Republic. A commando from this region was already on its way southwards, led by Commandant General Schoeman. It was a delicate situation that could easily have erupted in open warfare, in which lives would have been lost and passions would have been inflamed.

After negotiations, in which Kruger played a leading role, a commission was appointed to arrange a satisfactory settlement. Kruger reported the matter as follows:

> A commission was appointed to meet on the Vaal River to settle the difference. Here, although I did not at all approve of it, I was called upon to defend the action of my President, who was himself violently attacked. In the end a compromise was arrived at, and Pretorius relinquished his unjust claims.

However, the matter did not end there. A few years later, Pretorius, who wanted to unite both Boer republics into one state, was also elected president of the Orange Free State. When he left Pretoria to take up his new position, his deputy, the vice president, was appointed as acting president. However, the commandant general objected to the appointment and claimed that he should have been elevated to the position. The commandant general was the same Schoeman who a few years earlier had led the commando of northerners to oppose Pretorius and his supporters.

The events that followed were so serious – not to mention so complicated – that Kruger devoted a whole chapter of his memoirs to them. Opposing commandos faced off against each other, fortified positions were held in Pretoria and Potchefstroom, and shots were exchanged. Although there were some injuries and fatalities, generally the opposing parties circled around each other warily, with no one wanting to initiate a full-scale shooting war. Settlements were agreed and then abrogated or ignored. Finally, a general meeting of burghers pronounced that new office bearers should be elected and that a special court should be appointed to determine guilt and innocence in respect of the recent events; the court should be presided over by judges from the Orange Free State bench. However, the new president of the Orange Free State advised against this step because judicial action would result in too many sentences being handed down, which would again inflame passions and rekindle the smouldering antagonisms.

Finally, Kruger, who was now commandant general, proposed a solution that was accepted by all parties. Kruger wrote,

I now sought for a precedent for settling a matter of this kind, and at last discovered that an old jurist had laid down the principle that charges of rebellion in a country torn by civil war could, by general consent, be dismissed by a general amnesty, so long as the chief parties concerned were discharged from their official positions. The Volksraad so resolved, and peace was thus fully restored.

A general election was held, during which Kruger received a stamp of approval by being re-elected as commandant general by more than two-thirds of the voters.

Although Kruger commented in a matter-of-fact tone on his decisive intervention in the dispute, the wisdom and diplomatic skills that he displayed on this occasion would have contributed to his growing reputation as a leader.

Although the Sand River Convention was signed in 1852, which was about fourteen years after the first trekkers entered the region north of the Vaal River, as can be expected, the settlers did not sit around idly while waiting for approval of their status from Britain. With characteristic energy and purpose, they began to set up the structures and arrangements of an orderly society, modelled according to their desires and preferences. For instance, Paul Kruger stated that a year after he and his family members settled on the Highveld, when he was sixteen years of age, he was eligible to choose two farms 'like any other independent member of our community'. This suggests that there was already an agreement on how farms were measured and allocated, as well as a means of recording ownership.

Kruger noted that one farm was for grazing and one was for growing crops. As already seen, one of the urges that drove the Boers ever onwards, was that they were always searching for new places in which the upcoming generation could establish itself in the same manner as its elders had done. Moreover, the need for land increased exponentially, because most Boer families were large. For instance, Kruger records that although his first wife died in child-birth, his second wife had nine sons and seven daughters.

Little wonder, then, that it was not long before an expedition set out 'in order to colonise the conquered country'. According to Kruger, each member of the expedition was assured that he would receive another farm in the new piece of country. This was in 1845. During the previous year, a delegation of Boers had travelled to Delagoa Bay (now Maputo) to negotiate with the Portuguese authorities about the boundary between their territories. It was agreed that the Lebombo Mountains would be the boundary; these mountains still form part of the border between South Africa and Mozambique.

The expedition of 1845 went as far as the present-day town of Lydenburg, which is about 300 kilometres north-east of Pretoria, but did not establish a settlement there; instead, said Kruger, 'cattle-sickness and other evils determined us to return to the Magaliesberg, where I continued to live and acquired several farms by barter'. Until the threat of malaria and other diseases diminished, the Boers only occupied the Bushveld during winter, when they migrated there to provide their herds and flocks with grazing.

To Kruger and his compatriots, it was unremarkable that the Boers, who had only just arrived in the region, should be negotiating with a European country (Portugal) about the ownership of thousands of square kilometres of land. Although the Boers could, with justification, claim that the region between the Vaal River and the Magaliesberg was not only largely empty of inhabitants, but was also theirs by right of conquest, neither of these arguments applied to the Bushveld, which had long been inhabited, and about which the Boers knew very little. It was literally a case of claiming territory that had not even been explored or mapped, except in very broad outline.

The name of a town, Nylstroom, illustrates some Boers' ignorance about the region in which they had settled, as well as their Biblical fundamentalism. It is said that the name was given to the town because during the 1860s a party of Boers set off to trek all the way to the Holy Land. When they discovered a river running northwards, as well as a hill that looked like a pyramid, they consulted a map in one of their Bibles and, finding similarities, called the place Nylstroom (Nile River). Nylstroom, now renamed Modimelle, is about 140 kilometres north of Pretoria.

Of course, the Boers were not alone in claiming territory about which they knew very little, and which in any case was occupied by other people. Almost every European country was doing it or would soon be doing it. This point is worth noting because many British commentators had a superior attitude towards the Boers, who they portrayed as ignorant, ill-mannered, rough and crude. This attitude also extended to their opinions of the Boers' treatment of native people, with British commentators commonly depicting the Boers as cruel, violent and harsh compared to the British, who were portrayed as being more enlightened, more sympathetic and better-intentioned in their native policies.

However, not all British commentators thought that British policies and practices were superior or even defensible. For instance, as we have seen above, both Philip and Pringle held the opposite view. It is worth repeating Philip's condemnation of his countrymen's hypocrisy:

> While England boasts of her humanity, and represents the Dutch as brutes and monsters for their conduct towards the Hottentots and Bushmen, a narrow inspection into the proceedings which have taken place during the last two or three years, will bring to light a system, taken altogether, perhaps exceeding in cruelty anything recorded in the facts you have collected respecting the atrocities committed under the Dutch government.

As we have seen, in the same strain, Pringle wrote that he could not help beginning to suspect that his European countrymen were greater barbarians than the 'savage natives of Caffraria'. However, opinions like these were in the minority.

Before she went to live in the Transvaal during the late 1870s, the British-born Heckford was warned about the cruel ways of the Transvaal Boers. She was told that Boers had taken away black African babies from their mothers and, because the babies were too young to be reared, had thrown them into a heap and set fire to them. She was also told that nursing mothers had been shot in cold blood and, if they did not die immediately, had been left to linger in agony. Furthermore, she heard that children and been dragged from their mothers' arms, and the mothers had been shot if they pursued the attackers, pleading for mercy. Although these things might, or might not, have happened – and theft of native children certainly did occur – Heckford did not report that she experienced any such events during the time that she lived among the Transvaal Boers. However, as will be seen, she did report high-handed and crude behaviour towards servants.

Stanley expressed a typical, if right-of-centre, British-jingo opinion of the Boers when he wrote that 'their dull, dense, and dark minds are impenetrable to good sense'. Not unexpectedly, derogatory and dismissive views such as these became more and more common as the *uitlander* issue began to dominate British media and politics, and as the British public was groomed for war.

People holding the view that British policies and practices towards the natives were more enlightened, more good-willed and more principled would probably have justified it by referring to instances such as the abolition in the British Empire of enforced servitude and slavery, the attempts to conclude binding treaties with African tribes (rather than simply to enforce unilateral arrangements), the work of the missionaries, and the ostensibly non-racial constitution of the Cape Colony with its accompanying Cape Qualified Franchise. On the other hand, sceptics would point out that no matter how enlightened British policy appeared to be, the actual effect was dire: namely, that African groups such as the Xhosas and Zulus were squeezed into reserves of ever-decreasing size, where they became ever more impoverished, and were so restless and dissatisfied that they frequently engaged in rebellion or armed resistance. In addition, critics of British policies and practices could point to the fact that no Boer state ever presided over an event as tragic and traumatic as the Great Cattle Killing, during which hundreds of thousands of Xhosa people, frustrated and traumatised by colonial policies and pressures, died of starvation or were pauperised.

For a different view on enlightened British policies and practices towards native people, one can look across the Indian Ocean to Australia, where the treatment that the Aboriginal inhabitants of the continent received at the hands of the British authorities and settlers was atrocious and even genocidal. For instance, one can refer to what an early writer, John Eyre, had to say about the injurious treatment that the indigenous inhabitants of Australia were suffering at the hands of Europeans. By coincidence, Eyre's book was published in 1845, which was the same year as Kruger and his companions made their journey of exploration into the Bushveld and claimed the land as their own. It is also significant that Eyre's book was published less than sixty years after the first Europeans arrived to establish their settlement in what is now Sydney. Although sixty years seems like a relatively short period when seen against the long sweep of history, it was more than enough time for disaster to be inflicted on many Aboriginal groups.

Among others, Eyre made the following points:
• the presence of Europeans in Aboriginal territory was 'altogether an act of intrusion and aggression';
• Europeans occupied the best land, thus driving the indigenous people into inferior localities;
• the settlers had grievously injured Aboriginals 'by dispossessing them of their lands, by occupying their waters, and by depriving them of their supply of food'.

The result, wrote Eyre, was that 'They [the Aboriginals] are strangers in their own land, and possess no longer the usual means of procuring their daily subsistence.'

It needs to be remembered that the injustice, oppression and dispossession continued for at least another 100 years after these trenchant words were written. Dispossession and oppression of the Australian Aboriginals was a prolonged, all-encompassing and relentless process. In fact, Eyre was so shocked by the devastation and dispossession that he had witnessed, that he proposed the following:

Surely if we acknowledge the first principle of justice, or if we admit the slightest claims of humanity on behalf of these debased, but harshly treated people, we are bound, in honour and in equity, to afford them that subsistence which we have deprived them of the power of providing for themselves.

In other words, Eyre thought that the authorities and the settlers had treated the Aboriginals so badly, and had deprived them of so much, that justice and fairness required that the Aboriginals should be compensated for their grievous losses. Eyre's plea was ignored.

To return to the Boers: although the military successes of the Boers might suggest that the *volk* was almost monolithic and always united in sentiment and action, the reality was that its various constituents only came together in the face of danger and adversity. At other times, individualism and individual actions predominated. Stanley assessed the situation correctly when he wrote that Boer society was cemented by pressure from without rather than by cohesion from within. In agreement with this assessment, Eybers noted that, although the Boers united in their push to secure the country for themselves during their first years in their new territory, this cohesion did not last for long. Eybers wrote that once the land had been occupied, the various parties drew away from each other, and it was five years before a constitution could be settled. Furthermore, even while it was being settled, there were no fewer than three republics north of the Vaal River. Two of these republics, namely the South African Republic (the name adopted in 1853 for the entity that was based at Potchefstroom) and Zoutpansberg, joined together in 1858. Lydenburg joined two years later, after some constitutional amendments were made.

The constitution that was adopted in 1858 was true to the democratic sentiments that had carried the Boers so far, in time and space, from what they regarded as oppressive authority. The central principle of the constitution was that the people were the source of all authority, while other key aspects were that the executive was responsible to the legislature (in other words, the elected representatives of the people were paramount in decision-making), and that citizenship was restricted to white inhabitants who were members of the Dutch Reformed Church. (As stated earlier, partly as a concession to Paul Kruger, later this clause was amended to include members of the Reformed Church, or Doppers.) Immigrants could be admitted to citizenship after a prescribed period of residence, but only if they renounced their former citizenship and became members of the Dutch Reformed Church.

For the Transvaal Boers, their relationship with the natives was always a key concern. Fisher made an important point when he said of the defeat of the Matabele that this was the last fight in which the Transvaal Boers needed to defend their existence. All the native wars that followed were for the purpose of maintaining order and supremacy, and obtaining apprentices. In other words, after the Matabele were driven out of the territory that later became the Transvaal, although there were African groups that could resist Boer penetration to a greater or lesser extent, there were none that could mount a significant challenge to Boer domination of the region.

While the southern part of the Transvaal was almost unpopulated when the Boers occupied it, what was the situation in the rest of the region that the Boers were now claiming? Although it is difficult to get an accurate picture of the numbers and locations of the indigenous inhabitants during the early 1840s, there is one certainty, and that is the situation of the group known as the Bapedi (or Pedi). They had occupied the southern region until they were driven northwards by the Matabele; however, despite this dislocation, the Pedi remained reasonably intact and occupied the region that was known as Sekhukhuneland, which covered a large part of the area between the Magaliesberg and the Limpopo River, which later became the northern border of the Transvaal. Massie gave further details when he wrote that, after defeating Moselikatse, the Boers were masters of the situation, and proceeded to annex the whole territory formerly ruled by the Matabele. However, wrote Massie, there were too few of them to hold the whole country, so the original Bechuana-Basuto tribes who had been driven west and north by the Matabele invaders, now rapidly returned to occupy their former homes.

Becker agreed that after the Boers defeated the Matabele, they faced no challenges in occupying the southern part of the Transvaal. He wrote that all the territory that had been occupied by the Matabele, now became the Boers' by right of conquest. Here, said Becker, the Boers attained 'the realisation of their long-cherished dream – the establishment of a republican form of government, in accordance with the manners and traditions of their antiquated system'. Further evidence that the country in which the Boers first settled was thinly inhabited is found in Kruger's accounts of his hunting exploits. He wrote,

> During the first years of our settlement as well as during our wanderings it was our task to clear the recently acquired land of wild animals, which had hitherto roamed about unrestrained side by side with the wild races, and thus to protect our pastures...

Although Kruger wrote that the wild animals had roamed about 'side by side with the wild races' (that is, African tribes-people), there could not have been dense populations of these 'wild people' because, like the Boers, Africans kept large herds of cattle that competed with wild animals for grazing space.

When Kruger saw elephants for the first time in his life, it was near present-day Rustenberg, which is about 170 kilometres north-west of present-day Johannesburg. This is significant because elephants are usually killed or driven away wherever there are reasonably densely-populated human settlements, because of the damage that they do to crops and infrastructure, as well as because of the dangers that they pose to human beings. Supplementing the argument is the fact that it was in the same area that Kruger saw a rhinoceros for the first time.

14

Keeping Order

It is self-evident that their relationship with African groups was a major concern of the Transvaal Boers. The concern began more than half a century earlier on the eastern frontier of the Colony when, as we have seen, the advance parties of eastward-moving Boers first met the advance parties of westward-moving Xhosa-speaking tribes somewhere near the Great Fish River and the Zuurveld. Finally, also as we have seen, after a tumultuous period of mounting hostility and destruction, the issue escalated into one of the main causes of the Great Trek. Piet Retief forefronted the matter in his manifesto when he said that the Boers on the eastern frontier of the Colony could no longer endure 'a continual system of plunder...from the Kaffirs and other coloured classes...which has desolated the frontier districts, and ruined most of the inhabitants'. However, as subsequent history showed, it was almost a case of out of the frying pan into the fire, because in the years that immediately followed the exodus of trekkers from the Colony, the emigrants had numerous, deadly confrontations with the Zulus and Matabeles. These encounters increased the trekkers' determination always to have the upper hand and to be in control of the situation in their contacts and relationships with African groups. Not to be in control was to face destruction.

Being in control of the situation did not mean always conflicting with African groups. For instance, the Boer force that defeated Dingaan did so in alliance with dissident factions of the Zulu nation, while the Boers had African allies when they drove the Matabele away from the Highveld and carved out an area for settlement. Massie observed that in 1837, Moilo, the chief of the Baharutsi, assisted the Boers in driving out the Matabele, and assisted them a few years later in their wars against other tribes in the Transvaal. The Boers rewarded him by allowing him to reoccupy the land that his people had held originally. However, these were only short-term alliances of convenience: for instance, Mpande collaborated with the Boers because he wanted to eliminate Dingaan and seize the throne for himself, while the Baharutsi allied themselves with the Boers to regain their lost territory.

Short-term alliances aside, the long-term attitude of the Transvaal Boers towards African groups was one of continual wariness and caution. The surrounding African groups always greatly outnumbered the Boers, who felt that they would be overwhelmed if they did not maintain military ascendancy and political supremacy. The Boers' attitudes towards the Africans is encapsulated in Sarah Heckford's record of a conversation that she had with an old Boer woman who, wrote Heckford, 'was much interested in politics'. (This was during the late 1870s.) Remonstrating with the woman about the high price that she wanted for an ox, Heckford said, 'You are asking war prices; no one will give you ten pounds for an unsalted ox in peace times.' To this, the woman replied, 'We all mean to keep our oxen until the Kaffirs break out again: they are sure to break out – quite sure.'

As the woman's words suggest, armed clashes with various African tribes was a regular occurrence for the Transvaal Boers. For instance, the following are some of the clashes that Kruger recorded in his memoirs:

In 1852 there was an expedition against the Bechuana chief, Secheli, in which Kruger participated as a commandant. The reason, wrote Kruger, was that Secheli was protecting another chief, called Moselele, who had committed several murders in the South African Republic, and refused to deliver him up. (However, as seen below, David Livingstone attributed entirely different motives to the Boers.)

In the following year, Kruger was involved in an expedition against the chiefs Mapela and Makapan, in the Waterberg district, near

Makapanspoort, which is about 200 kilometres north of present-day Johannesburg. The expedition was mounted to avenge the murder of Herman Potgieter, brother of the late commandant general. This was a particularly acrimonious campaign because several Boer men and women had been tortured and killed in ways that suggested that ritual murders and cannibalism were involved. Makapan's people operated from fortified positions around deep caves and, with their opponents in an impregnable position, the Boers starved them out and hundreds died. At the end of the encounter, in Kruger's words, 'The children of the tribe, as soon as they fell into the hands of the Boers, were *ingeboekt* [booked in or registered], that is to say, portioned out among Boer families and kept under strict legal supervision until they came of age.' The commando then turned its attention to Mapela, Makapan's ally, but found that he and his people had fled.

Only a short time later, in December 1853, Kruger was on commando again, this time against the chief Montsioa, who lived about fifty kilometres from Potchefstroom, which was the Boer's capital at the time. The Boers were searching for stolen cattle, which they reclaimed after an armed clash.

Earlier, I referred to Kruger's hunting tales as corroborating evidence that the southern Transvaal region was sparsely populated when the Boers occupied it. However, the tales also revealed the remarkable bushcraft, horsemanship and marksmanship for which the Boers were famous, and which served them so well during both Anglo-Boer wars, among others. For instance, Kruger wrote,

> When I had passed the rhinoceros, I jumped from my horse to shoot him. I placed myself so that he had to pass me within ten paces; this would give me a good opportunity to hit him in a vulnerable place. One bullet killed him outright.

This feat was more remarkable for having been achieved with a muzzle-loading rifle.

Marksmanship of such high quality had been cultivated over many generations; for instance, reporting on a journey that he made to the outer districts of the Colony during the early 1800s, Borcherds wrote about the frontier Boers that their pride was to possess a good long gun or musket of large calibre, that could carry the ball with accuracy for a fair distance. He observed that he found it astonishing to see how precisely they made and regulated the sights to their guns. The next desirable object was a good horse, strong and trained for hunting. Fisher commented that the high quality of marksmanship derived from early training. The young Boer was sent out with only one or two cartridges, and he knew that he would get no food unless he came home with his game.

During one hunting expedition, Kruger's rifle exploded and almost destroyed one of his thumbs. He ignored the advice to have his hand amputated and treated the wound himself. First, he bathed it in turpentine after which he observed that 'the two joints of what was once my thumb had gone, but it appeared that it would still be necessary to remove a piece of bone'. He took up his knife, intending to perform the operation, but family members took it away from him. However, he persevered and, a little later, he cut across the ball of the thumb, removing' as much material as was necessary.' He said,

> The worst bleeding was over, but the operation was a very painful one. I had no means by me of deadening the pain, so I tried to persuade myself that the hand on which I was performing this surgical operation belonged to somebody else.

Then gangrene set in. After trying various remedies, he put his hand into the stomach of a freshly slaughtered goat. Kruger said, 'This Boer remedy succeeded, for when it came to the turn of the second goat, my hand was already easier and the danger much less.' The wound took more than six months to heal.

Although this might have been an extreme case, it does remind us that the Boers were famously hardy and self-reliant. Heckford noted similar qualities when she described a young family man named Du Plessis, who 'was known amongst his mates as a sure shot, a daring hunter, and a first-rate horseman…and withal a most diligent and energetic farmer'.

These characteristics were typical frontier qualities as identified by Turner who, writing about American history, noted that the frontier was a military training school, keeping alive the power of resistance to aggression and developing the stalwart and rugged qualities of the frontiersman. Also of relevance to the Boers was Turner's observation that the most important effects of the frontier were the promotion of democracy and the forging of individualism.

To return to the issue of the Boers and their attitude towards African groups, at least three main perspectives on the part of the Boers can be identified. In the first place, as the colonists (including many who were now Transvaal Boers) had done in the Cape Colony, they felt entitled to expand into, and occupy, whatever space they desired and no matter who also claimed the space. Usually, the Boers expanded their territories at the expense of African neighbours. As in the Colony, there was never a hint of doubt or hesitation about the matter. Only insurmountable external factors, such as natural barriers, political realities or military strength, constrained Boers from continually moving forwards and outwards in whatever direction seemed to offer desirable prospects.

The Boers maintained control over neighbouring African groups through a system of vassalage and tributary, in which chiefs acknowledged their allegiance to Boer authority, paid taxes, and kept the peace. For example, Theal (1886) commented on a letter that Commandant General Pretorius wrote to Chief Montsiwa during 1852. Pretorius wrote that his council had approved the boundary line between Boer territory and Montsiwa's territory; that he trusted that no encroachments would be made in future; and that Montsiwa should keep good rule and order amongst his people. Theal commented,

> All this looks very much as if Commandant General Pretorius regarded Montsiwa as an independent chief. But this was certainly not his view of the matter. The style of his letters is exactly the same as that in which he was in the habit of addressing all the petty chiefs in the country who were living under the farmers' [the Boers'] protection. We would term them vassals, but he chose to

call them allies. The boundary line he regarded as we would the boundaries of a native location in the Colony.

Theal's view is supported by an observation made by Heckford, who recounted an experience that she had when she was making a living as a *smous* (travelling salesman) at a place about 200 kilometres north of present-day Johannesburg, near where the ferocious clash between the Boers and Makapan and his people had taken place twenty-five years earlier. Heckford wrote that she soon realised that she would only be able to trade goods, not sell them, because the government was calling in taxes, and the local people were afraid of being short of money. If they could not pay, then their cattle would be taken at a ridiculously low value. From Heckford's observation, we see that the tribe, which had put up fierce resistance against the Boers twenty-five years earlier, was now subdued and subservient.

Secondly, as we have seen, to a significant extent the Boers' sense of entitlement arose from their sense of cultural superiority. They were Christian people, singled out and blessed by God, while the other groups were heathen. In addition, as is common with colonial enterprises, the Boers were convinced that they were bringing civilisation and progress to hitherto uncivilised, barbaric, and stagnant realms. As a number of commentators pointed out, in their relationships with 'Hottentot' and African people, the Boers, whose religious orientation was Old Testament rather than New, were guided by literal readings of the scriptures. For instance, their conduct in warfare often closely reflected the injunctions that were given to Israelite warriors in chapter twenty of the Book of Deuteronomy (amongst others):

> When you approach a city to wage war against it, offer it terms of peace. If it accepts your terms and submits to you, all the people found in it will become your slaves. If it does not accept terms of peace but makes war with you, then you are to lay siege to it. The Lord your God will deliver it over to you and you must kill every single male by the sword. However, the women, little children, cattle, and anything else in the city – all its plunder – you may

take for yourselves as spoil. You may take from your enemies the plunder that the Lord your God has given you.

Thirdly, there was a practical aspect to the Boers' attitude towards African groups, namely that they needed labourers. For instance, Kruger stated unambiguously that, after occupying their new territory north of the Vaal River, 'The first care of the new settlers was to secure reliable labour and to induce the black inhabitants of the country to undertake it.' One method of obtaining labour was to offer inducements over and above wages by granting labourers the right to use part of a farm for their own purposes. Becker noted that the families that were working on a farm were given a few acres of ground to till for their own use, and for their houses. The farmer paid reduced wages as compensation for the use of the land.

However, the Boers also satisfied their need for labour in other ways. Earlier, we saw that Kruger wrote that, after a clash between a Boer commando and an African group, the children of the tribe were captured and were *ingeboekt* or portioned out among Boer families until they came of age. The system of booking in or registering captive children, which originated in the frontier districts of the Cape Colony during the late eighteenth century, was common in the Transvaal. The Boers claimed that because the children were orphans, they (the Boers) were doing them a favour by providing the helpless youngsters with a home, protection, and the means of survival. The children were called apprentices; males were indentured until the age of twenty-five, while females were released at twenty-one years of age.

The *ingeboekt* system was based on the indenture system that was widely practised in European countries and their colonies from the Middle Ages until about the mid-nineteenth century, if not later. In fact, echoes of the system are still found in some of the rules and procedures that govern some apprenticeships today.[10] Essentially, under indenture, in return for benefits, youths voluntarily bound themselves over to others for a specified period. A common form of indenture was the one in which passage from the Old World to the New was paid for by indenture. In return for payment for the passage, the youth would commit himself/herself to work for the new master for a specified period, during which he/she was often provided with board and lodging and might also learn new skills or a useful trade. The indenture was legally registered and enforceable. In addition, it could be bought and sold. However, this did not amount to slavery, because the person was never owned by a master, and the indenture ended at the end of the contracted period.

In significant ways, the Boer form of indenture differed from the more widely practised system. Firstly, it was not voluntary, because the subjects were captives who had no say in the matter. Secondly, it involved young children. In fact, some of them were very young. Thirdly, unlike the indenture elsewhere, under the Boer form, because the subjects were so young and helpless, there was no reciprocity. In other words, the advantages and benefits were all on the side of the masters, because the subjects did not, and could not, agree to the terms and conditions under which they would serve.

Livingstone, who called the system slavery, claimed that there was a shrewd reason for seizing children, namely that while it was difficult to find and reclaim a runaway slave because there was no fugitive slave law in Africa, if a child was stolen, he would forget his mother tongue and original home, and therefore would not be likely to run away.

Clearly, this system was open to massive abuse. Critics claimed that forays by Boers against African groups, which were ostensibly undertaken to settle boundary disputes, to quell rebellions or dissidence or to extract taxes, were mainly intended to acquire cattle and indentured labour. For instance, Massie wrote that a raid served a double purpose. Even those Boers who did not want to take part in a raid to capture slaves could seldom resist the story that a tribe was planning an uprising, because all Boers knew that cattle could be captured during an expedition. A double purpose was thus served by the raid. Boers with good consciences only took cattle, while those with less refined consciences took the children as apprentices, who, said Massie, 'were brought up to perform all the duties of the emancipated slaves'. Massie also claimed that the Boers used indenture to weaken the power of tribes that might oppose them because capturing children contributed to breaking up a tribe to nullify it as a threat.

Writing in 1871, Chesson repeated the criticism by stating that, in fact, the Boers created the misery which they claimed to alleviate. Furthermore, he claimed that not only were commandos organized specifically for capturing children to be used as slaves, but that traffic in slaves was practised all over the ZAR, with the prices varying from twelve to twenty pounds per head. Chesson's assertions might have been exaggerated because, as an Englishman who was active in movements that opposed slavery and promoted the welfare of Aborigines, he hoped to influence the British government to take action against the Transvaal Boers on the grounds that they had violated the provisions of the Sand River Convention by practising slavery and slave-trading. Nevertheless, his claims do broadly agree with those of other commentators.

Reflecting their position as non-citizens and lesser creatures, Africans who worked within Boer territory were subjected to discriminatory laws and treatment. For instance, an employer had the right to flog an errant African employee, as described in Heckford's account of an incident in which one of her African employees was found guilty of stealing goods from her. At the court hearing, which was held alongside Heckford's wagon, the magistrate sentenced the guilty party to twenty-five lashes but stated that he could escape the sentence by paying a fine of three pounds. However, Heckford, who had lost goods to the value of about fifty pounds, insisted that the sentence should be carried out. What followed was a form of summary justice, as seen in Heckford's description:

> They were round him in a minute, those Boers and Hendrick, like hounds round a fox. They tripped him up, they pulled him about and yelped over him; Jan Steen was the foremost. It was a disgusting spectacle. 'Look here,' cried I, in a rage, 'if you don't leave that man alone I'll send every one of you away from my wagon; he is to be punished – not tortured; stand back all of you.'
> ... He got his five-and-twenty...

Another law that applied only to Africans was the prohibition on buying and consuming liquor, unless an African had permission from his master. In addition, there was a form of pass control, in the sense that there was a limit to the number of African that one employer could employ. On the other hand, as seen in the almost unrestricted influx of outsiders during mining booms, there were no apparent restrictions on entry by people of European background.

15

Relationships

During the Boers' expedition against the Bechuana chief, Secheli, an incident that involved David Livingstone was much-debated at the time. Even today, it is a subject of controversy among historians. This is how Kruger reported the incident:

> After hostilities were concluded, Commandant Scholtz sent up to the house of Livingstone, the English missionary, which was not far from the Kaffir town. Here Theunis Pretorius found a complete workshop for repairing guns, and a quantity of materials of war which Livingstone was storing for Secheli. This was a breach of the Sand River Convention of 1852, which prescribed that neither arms nor ammunition should be supplied to the Kaffirs, and that they should not be permitted to provide either for themselves. Scholtz accordingly confiscated the missionary's arsenal…

Kruger concluded his account by saying that, because of the incident, Livingstone verbally abused the Boers throughout England, and slandered them as enemies of the missionaries and cruel persecutors of Africans.

The incident reflected the Boers' deep concern that their African neighbours should not have access to firearms. They feared that with fire-arms, numerical superiority would be translated into military superiority. However, Kruger disingenuously explained the Boers' determination to keep fire-arms out of African hands as arising from their concern not to give Britain any reason for accusing them of violating treaties and thus give Britain an excuse to annul the Sand

River Convention which, said Kruger, 'guaranteed the liberty of the emigrants north of the Vaal'.

Livingstone described the incident differently. He wrote that when 400 Boers attacked the Bakwains, they boasted that 'the English had given up all the blacks into their power' and that the British had agreed that the Boers could launch attacks to prevent supplies of ammunition from coming into the Bechuana country. The Boers killed many adults and carried off 200 schoolchildren (into slavery, stated Livingstone). The Bakwains defended themselves with determination until they were able to flee into the mountains after nightfall. Because the Bakwains killed several attackers (Livingstone said, 'the very first ever slain in this country by Bechuanas'), Livingstone was accused of having taught the tribespeople to kill Boers. In addition, wrote Livingstone, stores and cattle belonging to English hunters were stolen, his library was vandalised, his medicines were destroyed, and the family's furniture and clothing were carried away. (Livingstone and his family were absent from the settlement at the time.)

Livingstone claimed that the Boers' main purpose in attacking Koboleng was to prevent traders and missionaries from travelling into the interior along what is now the main route northwards through Gaborone, the capital of Botswana. In addition, he alluded to slave-gathering as a motive.

Other questions and issues can be raised around the incident. For instance, by saying that the Boers '[boasted] that the English had given up all the blacks into their power', Livingstone was clearly implying that, at least by some interpretations, the Bechuana country was not covered by the Sand River Convention. Secondly, Livingstone questioned the right of the Boers and the British to decide unilaterally for autonomous African groups. Thirdly, Livingstone stated that the workshop and war materials to which the Boers objected, were used by British hunters and not by the Bechuana people.

Here, it should be noted that Livingstone was outspoken in his criticism of the Transvaal Boers not only because he was an advocate of even-handed treatment for Africans, especially for the Bakwain people amongst whom he had laboured, but also because he passionately and single-mindedly devoted so much of his life to eliminating slavery and slave-trading from Africa. Accordingly, he disliked agreements like the Sand River Convention that were designed to give military superiority to white people by denying Africans access to firearms.

Although Kruger said of the Koboleng incident that 'the Boers were neither opposed to the mission nor enemies of the natives', the truth was that the Boers were extremely wary of allowing missionaries into either their territory or the territory of any of the subservient tribes on their borders. This was not a new concern because, as we have seen, the Boers had been suspicious of missionaries for a long time, since the days of Van Der Kemp, Read and John Philip, during the first decades of the nineteenth century. As seen earlier, Retief raised the issue in his manifesto when he stated that an unjustifiable odium had been cast upon the Boers by persons who operated under the cloak of religion. As Retief stated, the antipathy of the Boers arose not only from what the missionaries said and did in the field, but from the fact that they directly influenced Imperial policies towards the Colony. According to most of the settlers (both Boer and non-Boer), these policies not only promoted an unacceptable equality between white and non-white people, but also paved the ways for rebellions and incursions.

Self-evidently, there were significant differences between the world views of the Boers and the perspectives of most of the missionaries. As Fisher said,

> Livingstone…could not understand how the Boers could reconcile their practice of slave-raiding with their profession of Christianity. To his amazement, as he wrote to a friend at home, 'their Church is, and has always been, the great bulwark of slavery, cattle-lifting, and Kaffir marauding.'

These words touched on several key issues. Firstly, there was the view that Christianity is incompatible with slave-owning and slave-trading; underlying the anti-slavery position was the belief that all human beings were worthy of respect and had innate rights, irrespective of their origins, cultures or backgrounds. Broadly, the missionaries espoused humanism, which was a view that gained traction during the Enlightenment and was boosted by the influence of revolutionary ideas. Although it was contested ground, in Britain the humanists achieved great victories when slave-trading in the Empire was abolished in 1808 and when slavery itself was abolished in 1833. However, while humanists regarded these and similar measures as great victories, the Boers regarded them as retrogressive and abhorrent.

Clearly, humanism was almost diametrically opposed to the particularistic views of the Boers, who regarded themselves as uniquely Christian and therefore inherently superior and entitled to dominate and exploit those who belonged to lesser races. To put it broadly, where the Christianity of the Boers was more orientated to the Old Testament, the Christianity of many of the missionaries was more orientated to (some interpretations of) the New Testament. Many missionaries would have agreed with the sentiment that is expressed in the New Testament Book of Galatians, where the Apostle Paul wrote that 'There is neither Jew nor Greek, there is neither slave nor free man, there is neither male nor female; for you are all one in Christ Jesus.' However, the Boer position on these matters was expressed in that part of the constitution of the ZAR that proclaimed that 'the people will admit of no equality of persons of colour with white inhabitants, neither in Church nor State' (as cited by Becker).

The antagonism and tension that often existed between the Boers and missionaries can be seen in a memorial that representatives of three mission societies submitted to the special commissioner of the British government, who was investigating the viability of the continued existence of the Orange River Sovereignty during 1853. The three societies were the London Society, the Berlin Society, and the Paris Society, and Theal reported that they complained about the conduct of the Boers toward the natives and about the destruction by the Boers of five mission stations. They stated that they were convinced that the attacks were unprovoked, and arose from the love of plunder, the lust for power and the desire of the Boers to obtain unpaid labour. Furthermore, wrote Theal, the missionaries complained that the system pursued by the Boers towards the tribes under their control was reducing them all to a state of servitude which amounted to slavery. Unsurprisingly, the Boer's representative refuted and rejected all these charges. While he acknowledged that most of the incidents had occurred, he claimed that other parties had been responsible or that the events had not occurred as stated.

At this remove, it is difficult to say where the truth lay, or even to discern what might have happened in each case. However, one thing is certain, namely that the memorial would have strengthened the antipathy of the Boers towards missionaries and would have fortified their determination to exclude missionaries and mission influences from their territories. In fact, as Fisher recorded, there was a deliberate attempt to exclude not only missionary influence, but all external influence, from the Transvaal. Fisher wrote that five mission stations were broken up and a trader was fined 500 rix-dollars for publishing a description of the road to Lake Ngami which, the Boers feared, would lead to an increase in hunters and traders on the western edge of their territory. Furthermore, a law was passed to prevent Englishmen or Germans from holding land in the Transvaal, and another to prohibit mining and working with minerals. He concluded that

> Every attempt, in short, was made to keep the outside world ignorant about the doings of the Republic; and for some dozen years the Boers were quite successful in this policy of seclusion.

I can find only one further mention of missionaries and their work in connection with the Transvaal Boers. This reference is to John Mackenzie, a missionary of the London Missionary Society (of which John Philip was a member), which was the Boers' greatest bête noire amongst missionary societies. Mackenzie was instrumental in having large parts of Bechuanaland declared a British protectorate, claiming this would shield the Tswana people from Boer incursions. The Boers deeply resented this move, not only because of the accusations of racism and slave-dealing that prompted it, but also because it restricted their expansion on the western borders of the Transvaal.

Praagh described the relationship of the Boers towards missionaries by writing that although the constitution did not allow the equality of coloured persons with white inhabitants, whether in Church or State, the promulgation of the gospel among Africans was allowed, subject to certain precautions against teaching false doctrines. In reality, said Praagh, the Boers put every obstacle in the way of the missionaries, while their own Dutch Reformed Church did not at all engage in missionary work. Fisher agreed with this assessment and stated that one of the first steps taken by the first President of the ZAR, Marthinus Wesssel Pretorius, was to close the country to visitors, especially to those who were suspected of being interested in the education of Africans. Missionaries were the most unwelcome of all.

16

Size and Isolation

The Transvaal Boers comprised a numerically small society. For instance, Theal estimated that the Transvaal was occupied by about 5,000 European families in 1852. Considering the size of families at that time, and recognising the degree of latitude of the estimation, 5,000 families would probably amount to between 25,000 and 35,000 men, women and children. Writing about twenty years later, Chesson estimated that there was a lower number of Boers, namely 20,000 to 30,000. However, for political reasons, Chesson was probably inclined to underestimate. Whatever the actual number, this was a small number of inhabitants for a large tract of country which Chesson estimated to encompass about 100,000 square miles. To put the size of the Boer community into perspective, nowadays a medium-size country town in most developed countries has about the same number of people, namely a population of between 25,000 and 40,000.

Allowing for natural increase over the years, a corresponding number was reported by Becker, who stated that in an imperfect census that was taken in 1876, it was estimated that the white population was about 45,000, and the coloured or native portion about 300,000 although probably fewer Africans than whites lived within the boundaries of European occupation. Of the whites, probably about 35,000 or 40,000 lived in the rural districts and 5,000 in the towns. Of significance in view of the later dispute over *uitlanders* (foreigners) was the estimate that British citizens predominated in the towns and mining areas, while the population was almost exclusively British in the gold fields. The proportion of the population involved in mining would have been quite small, because the great influx only began ten years later when the Witwatersrand mines were opened. Becker's estimate show that the population was overwhelmingly rural, and that comparatively few natives could reside within the areas that were reserved for white occupation. The reference to a coloured or native portion of about 300,000 must have applied to people who were living in border areas that the Boers regarded as subservient to their authority and control, but that were not actually occupied by them.

A somewhat more reliable indication of the size of the population about twenty-five years later is provided by the fact that 14,864 votes were recorded in the presidential election of 1893 (cf. Fisher). The franchise was restricted to adult males so, presuming that there was about an equivalent number of adult females, there would have been a total of about 30,000 adults. Based on this figure, a rough estimate would suggest a total Boer population of about 75,000 in 1893.

Writing in 1881, Aylward, a British citizen who lived in the Transvaal for several years, thought that the developments that had taken place within a relatively short time were remarkable in view of the small size of the population. He wrote that

> the Boers occupy an extensive country: and on its surface they have wrought improvements, which, compared with their numbers, are sufficiently astonishing. There are roads – and very good roads – everywhere. There are churches, courts, and jails in sufficient number; and…the extent of ground under cultivation is very great.

He estimated that there were about 7,000 families making their livings on farms and termed it little less than miraculous that 'the Boers had succeeded, in so few years…in planting the features of a successful civilisation over 130,000 square miles of country'. (Aylward was a mercurial Irishman who was rather more pro-Boer than the British authorities in South Africa liked, so his praise for developments in the Transvaal might have been somewhat rose-tinted.)

Aylward's estimate that there were about 7,000 Boer families would suggest a total population of about 45,000, which generally agrees with other estimates that have been cited above.

Heckford provided an amused illustration of just how closely bound the Boer community was, in both social and family relationships, when she wrote that she visited an old woman named Nell. Heckford wrote that the woman was

> related to the De Clercs and Engelsbergs in some inextricable manner, as is often the case with Boer relationships. This is natural, when it is the custom for people of both sexes to marry so often as they do in Boer-land, for each succeeding wife to call her actual husband's mother 'ma,' her former husband's or husbands' mother 'ma' and her husband's former wives' mothers 'ma.' The husbands observe the same rule, one that includes the various fathers as well, who are called 'pa' by a variety of people hardly related to them according to our ideas. The relationships become still more bewilderingly intricate, when one considers that the 'pa' and 'ma' may marry half-a-dozen times themselves, and may thus multiply their children's fathers or mothers, and grandfathers, and grandmothers to an appalling extent. I once made, or at least attempted, a calculation of the number of grandmothers a Boer might have, but I felt that to grapple with the subject was to court insanity, and so desisted.

The high degree of individualism, the small size of the population, and its widely scattered nature, partly explain the individualism of the early settlers. For instance, as Fisher recorded, in 1852 there were about 5,000 European families in the country who were spread over four districts, each of which was governed by a commandant, each being of equal rank with the others. The *Volksraad* of the Transvaal made this arrangement to appease the jealousies that existed among the leaders, of whom the two most important were Potgieter and Pretorius. Each of the four jurisdictions had a small population of about only 7,500 to 8,500 people on average. It was only after about fifteen years of settlement that all the various groups finally united in one political entity, which was known as the South African Republic (ZAR). Lydenburg, which was founded in 1848, was the last republic to surrender its independence when it joined the ZAR in 1860.

With the overwhelming number of Boers making their living as pastoralists and agriculturalists on large farms, there were comparatively few towns. Those that did exist were far apart, small and basic. As an example, a description of Lydenburg soon after it was founded stated that the central feature of the town plan was the *Kerkplein* or Church Square around which were built the *landdrost*'s office, a small church and a simple schoolhouse. The author described the schoolhouse as primitive, with the children sitting on the floor. The other major design feature was the *Markplein* or Market Square, which not only served as the marketplace but also provided a place for families to set up their encampments during the quarterly *Nagmaal*[11] or Holy Communion gathering. We see that the towns were centres for the administration of law (through the *landdrost*), for worship, for some formal education (but mainly for town children) and for trade.

As we have seen, membership of a Reformed Church was an essential requirement for citizenship in the ZAR. *Nagmaal* was a central event in the church calendar: at this quarterly event, the widely scattered members of a congregation gathered to worship together and to take Holy Communion. However, these gatherings were much more than merely occasions for worship. One writer described a typical *Nagmaal* gathering like this: a few days before the occasion, farmers and their families out-spanned their wagons in neat rows on the Church Square and pitched one or more tents next to them; however, some well-off Boers had town houses that they used on these occasions. *Nagmaal* was much more than a religious occasion, because it also allowed families and friends to visit and socialise with each other. So many people attended the event that to accommodate all the members of the congregation, numerous church services would be held, beginning on Saturday afternoon and going all through Sunday. On Sunday evening, there would be a gathering of the congregation, at which the minister and the church committee would lead a discussion about the affairs of the church, and at which any member of the congregation was free to ask questions, make suggestions, and deliver criticism. Often a bazaar would also be held during the weekend, to raise money for the church.

In view of the central place of religion in Boer identity, it is significant that the quarterly *Nagmaal* gathering, which was one of the strongest and most enduring of the Boers' group-bonding, identity-affirming acts, was related to the church.

By now, we have a picture of a society that was widely scattered and vulnerable, but that was bound together in common identity by shared beliefs, practices, and habits, such as their strong faith, the traditions and practices of their church (from which, largely, arose their democratic and republican ideals), their desire to be self-governing, their rugged individualism, their common pastoral and agricultural way of life, their sense of their God-given place in the world, and their shared history. However, to maintain their identity, they needed barriers; without the barriers, their identity would be infiltrated, undermined and dissipated, if not almost entirely obliterated.

Firstly, the barriers were physical, in the sense that they exercised rigid control over their borders and their neighbours, allowing a limited number of Africans to work within their territory, but not to own land or have rights. (Becker wrote that 'According to the law of 1873, every farmer is allowed to employ ten Kaffirs free of tax, who are bound to him by a yearly contract.')

Secondly, the barriers were political, in the sense that only white people who were members of a Reformed church could be citizens and have rights, which included the right to elect office bearers and political representatives.

Thirdly, the barrier was intellectual, in the sense that, with little or no formal education, no libraries, very little penetration of media such as newspapers and magazines, and an almost hermetically sealed belief in the rightness of their actions and identity, there was neither much exposure to ideas from the wider world, nor much interest in them. In this regard, Fisher was not being too ungenerous when he noted that the Boers of the Transvaal had hardly changed during two centuries, whether in manners, customs, or education. The isolation was intensified by the distance from markets and the difficulties of transportation, which discouraged travel and wider social contacts.

Fourthly, the barrier was spiritual, in the sense that they believed that they had a God-given calling and identity which not only conferred on them membership of the elect and made them superior to those who believed otherwise, but also required that they should strive to protect their revealed truth and divinely ordained status. In this regard, the embargo on missionary activity was an important factor in preserving their intellectual and spiritual isolation. On the intellectual level, it prevented exposure to humanist ideas that were directly contradictory to the particularism of the Boers, while on the spiritual level, it not only prevented exposure to religious teachings that were inclusive and universalist, but also prevented Africans from being converted to Christianity and thus being raised to a spiritual level that was equivalent to that of the Boers.

Of course, like most people everywhere when they are going about their ordinary, day-to-day lives, most Boers were not regularly or continuously concerned with great matters of politics and ideology. If there were no immediate dangers or alarms at hand, their concerns were with getting and spending, with loving and begetting, and with all the rest of life's regular and mundane matters. Heckford portrayed the ordinary life of a Transvaal farmer during the late 1870s when she compared the thoughts and motives of a European-born farmer with those of an Africander (that is, African-born) farmer; the latter, wrote Heckford,

> thinks of all his possessions as things that he has perhaps won by toil, but with which, now that he has them, he is contented, looking for nothing beyond. His crops will realize a price which will enable him to live as he is living...his cows will calve, his ewes will lamb, and he will every year mark some of their little ones for his own little ones, so that when they are men and women they,

too, will have flocks and herds, without having to take away from their old father.

This is an appropriate place at which to cite Fisher's comprehensive assessment of Boer character. He wrote that the average Boer, like most human beings, was a combination of good and evil. His best qualities were his stubborn perseverance in the face of difficulty and danger, his genuine family affection, his equally genuine though narrow and antiquated religious spirit, his determination never to endure injustice, and his hospitality to guests of whom he approved. His worst faults were his brutal treatment of Africans, his defect in political honesty, and his curious lack of passion for cleanliness and industry. In addition, said Fisher, Boers were usually opposed to progress.

One of the most notable features of the constitution of the ZAR was the fact that, as the elected representative of the burghers, the legislature was supreme. Its laws could not be overruled, reinterpreted or rescinded by any other person or body, such as, for instance, the president or a court. Another notable feature was the fact that the president was directly elected and, wrote Eybers,

> As the chosen man of the people, the President was in a very strong position. He became the leading figure in the executive as well as in the legislature, though he did not select his executive, had no veto on legislation, and could not dissolve the *Volksraad*... The President's position was due to the stress and danger to which the country was always exposed.

A controversy involving a president precipitated a national crisis that exposed fault lines in the nation and led to the first armed clash with British troops since a Boer force had exchanged fire with Sir Harry Smith's force during the days of the short-lived Orange River Sovereignty about twenty years earlier. In addition, by giving the Boers an inflated sense of their military and strategic strength, it possibly contributed to the onset of the (Second) Anglo-Boer War, in which the nation was defeated and laid waste.

The episode began when diamonds were discovered in the region where the Orange and Vaal Rivers join. Recognising the economic value of the region, various parties laid claim to it. These included the ZAR, the Orange Free State, the Griquas under Waterboer, and even a group of (mainly British) miners, who set up a short-lived independent state in the diamond fields. Under the Keate Award, the British government recognised the Griqua claim and soon afterwards annexed the territory as part of the Cape Colony. Praagh described the effect on the Transvaal as follows:

> Governor Keate's award gave to the tribes the independence they claimed, and even took from the Government at Pretoria a large district that had been occupied by white people ever since the great migration. As soon as the award was known President Pretorius was obliged to resign, for the *Volksraad* maintained that he had exceeded his authority in making the agreement with the High Commissioner and declared that they were not bound by his action.

The Boers felt that they had been hoodwinked and outmanoeuvred and, wrote Praagh, the result was that they considered that they needed a clever man at the head of affairs, who could negotiate successfully with the British authorities.

This led to the Reverend Thomas Francois Burghers being elected as the new president. It is difficult to understand why he was elected, because apart from his qualifications of being South African-born, Dutch-speaking, and a minister of the Dutch Reformed Church, he did not have much in common with most Transvaal Boers. In the first place, being both born and resident in the Cape Colony, he was not a burgher of the Transvaal. In the second place, despite being a well-qualified *predikant* of the Reformed church with a doctorate in theology from the University of Utrecht in the Netherlands, he had undisguised liberal and rationalist views. In fact, his views had put him so much at odds with the church in the Cape that he was charged with heresy and suspended from practising as a minister; he was only re-admitted after a Supreme Court decision. This was hardly a profile that was compatible with that of most Transvaal Boers, who were, of course, not only deeply conservative (in fact, the very opposite of liberal and rationalist) but were also Biblical fundamentalists.

In his memoirs, Kruger wrote that President Burghers

> was without doubt a man of keen intelligence and of very great gifts. He endeavoured without delay to improve the government of the country and to enter into commercial relations with foreign countries. Another favourite project of his was the construction of a railway from Lorenzo Marques to Pretoria, and he personally undertook a journey to Europe to borrow money for this purpose.

However, despite these complimentary words, Kruger not only developed into one of Burgher's most redoubtable opponents but was foremost amongst those who were responsible for his political demise.

On the negative side was the fact that Burghers' views differed too much from those of most of the burghers. As Kruger said, the republic was not ready to accept his advanced ideas. The differences were so great that Burghers rapidly lost popularity because, as Kruger observed, 'his liberal views regarding religion soon won him a host of adversaries'. Another difference with the burghers was the fact that the president's plans for a railway were not matched by the financial resources of the ZAR, for the burghers did not like to pay much income tax, if any at all. However, as Kruger noted, it was the Sekukuni War of 1876 that finally sank Burghers' presidency.

The causes of the war were the usual ones of disagreements over land and cattle, together with the Boers' need to keep order on their borders and maintain their dominance. For some reason, President Burghers decided to lead the expeditionary force even although there is no evidence that he had any military experience. The chances of success were further reduced when Burghers and Kruger fell out with each other. Kruger thought that, as commandant general, he should lead the expedition, so he refused to go when Burghers insisted on accompanying the commando. He told Burghers, 'I cannot lead the commando if you come; for with your merry evenings in the laager and your Sunday dances, the enemy will shoot me even if I am protected by a wall; for God's blessing will not rest on our expedition.' Perhaps Kruger should rather have said, 'I have years of experience of fighting in all kinds of situations while you, François Burghers, have none. This expedition is sure to end badly.'

The campaign failed, and the main Boer force withdrew, leaving small numbers of men in various forts, from which they harassed Sekukuni's people and eventually forced him to agree to a settlement of sorts. However, the campaign not only strained the ZAR's resources but damaged Burghers' reputation and caused dissension. His reputation nose-dived even further when he levied a special tax of five pounds on every burgher to pay for the costs of the outposts. Kruger considered that the tax was unlawful because it was imposed without the consent of the *Volksraad*, and a considerable number of the burghers refused to pay. This controversy further eroded the relationship between the president and Burghers.

17

Annexation and After

At this time, the British government wanted to forge a confederation of South African states that would include the two British colonies and the two Boer states. However, the independence-loving Boer states rejected the move. During 1877, with the Transvaal in a seemingly weak position, Sir Theophilus Shepstone, the British Secretary for Native Affairs in Natal, annexed the Transvaal for Britain.

Fitzpatrick described the Boer position as follows:

> The Boers were quite unable to pay the taxes necessary to self-government and the prosecution of the *Kaffir* wars. The Treasury was empty – save for the much-quoted 12s. 6d. The Government £1 blue-backs [bank notes] were selling at one shilling. Civil servants' salaries were months in arrears. The President himself… (had) not only drawn no salary, but had expended his private fortune, and incurred a very heavy liability, in the prosecution of the unsuccessful Secocoeni war.

Praagh stated that the situation was so dire that there were no public offices worthy of the name, the treasury was always empty, and the salaries of the officials were seldom paid.

To this catalogue of troubles should be added that it was suspected that King Cetawayo of the Zulus, who was rearming and reorganising his warriors, was planning to invade the Transvaal. The British claimed to be concerned that a move by Cetawayo could upset the balance of power in Southern Africa. In addition, they claimed that Sekukuni's ongoing resistance was an encouragement to other African groups to rebel against European control.

Shepstone seems to have believed that most Boers tolerated the annexation, even if they did not accept it with enthusiasm. However, the initial lack of determined action against the annexation was partly because the Transvaal was in a political hiatus when Shepstone made his move. The president's term of office had expired, and it looked as if Kruger would defeat Burghers by a large majority in the coming election. However, the annexation sidelined the election and Burghers, who accepted the annexation to resolve what he regarded as a political mess, remained in charge. Kruger wrote, 'Before the election took place, however, the British flag waved over the once-free Republic.'

Although Burghers was still exercising the presidential functions, he was openly at odds with most members of the *Volksraad* and with the Executive Council. For instance, Fitzpatrick recorded that Burghers said to the members of the *Volksraad*,

> I would rather be a policeman under a strong Government than the President of such a State. It is you – you members of the Raad and the Boers – who have lost the country, who have sold your independence for a *soupe* (a drink). You have ill-treated the natives, you have shot them down, you have sold them into slavery, and now you have to pay the penalty. We should delude ourselves by entertaining the hope that matters would mend by-and-by. It would only be self-deceit. I tell you openly, matters are as bad as they ever can be; they cannot be worse.

Although Fitzpatrick, with his pro-British leaning, probably embellished Burghers' speech, there is no doubt that Burghers had not only lost patience with the *Volksraad*, but also despaired of the task. He left the ZAR soon afterwards, never to return.

Although Shepstone was encouraged by the demonstrations of support that he received, Kruger dismissed them as representing the views of only a small minority. He wrote,

> A large majority of the burghers who lived in the plains were, as has already been stated, dissatisfied with the President's government, while the inhabitants of the villages, who consisted

almost entirely of foreigners, and of whom a large number were not even burghers, were contented with Burghers' rule, above all because they expected great things from the proposed railway.

As Kruger stated, support for the annexation came almost entirely from the non-burgher, urbanised part of the population. This division between 'country (the burghers who lived in the plains)' and the villages, namely the foreigners who had come to the Transvaal for business and financial reasons, ominously presaged the *uitlander* crisis that would play a major role in precipitating the disastrous war of 1899–1902.

Kruger, who had been appointed as vice-president under a temporary arrangement, took over leadership after Burghers left the country. He led an unsuccessful delegation to Britain to protest the annexation and, upon returning home, he facilitated the holding of a plebiscite, which was not recognised by the British authorities, to attest opinion about the annexation. Kruger reported that his committee met on April 1878 and found 6,591 petitions against the annexation, with 587 in favour. Kruger was satisfied that this showed overwhelming opposition to the annexation, because there were only about 8,000 voters in the ZAR and, he observed, he was sure that more opponents of the annexation had not been able to attend the meetings at which the petitions were signed. As subsequent events proved, the clear majority of the burghers were, indeed, opposed to the annexation. However, even with this evidence at hand, the second delegation that Kruger led to Britain was also a failure.

In 1879, two key events occurred that paved the way for the Boers to escalate their resistance to the annexation. The first event was the British defeat of the Zulus, and the second was the British defeat of Sekukuni. (However, Kruger stated dismissively that because the Boers had brought Sekukuni to the brink of defeat, the British-led force merely had to administer the *coup de grâce*.) With these two opponents out of the way, the Boers felt more secure and were emboldened to begin to reclaim their independence.

Kruger played a leading role in all the events that led up to the outbreak of hostilities. His memoirs relate a series of petitions to the British authorities, meetings with the authorities in various places, and protest meetings attended by thousands of burghers. Although many burghers were impatient with the slow pace of the negotiations, Kruger and other leaders counselled caution and delay, avoiding violence until all avenues had been exhausted.

Heckford relates events from the perspective of a British citizen in the Transvaal. Because of her work as a *smous* (that is, a travelling salesperson), moving around in country areas and dealing with many customers, she was well acquainted with many Boers. She wrote, 'There was beginning to be a feeling of insecurity in Pretoria. There was nothing to be seen but people felt that the air was electric. I was pretty sure that the Boers would fight…' Heckford also reported a conversation that she had with an elderly Boer who told her that the Boers were not afraid of British cannons. He explained,

> We don't fight as you do… What is the use of cannon against men who scurry round singly on horseback, and who shoot at you from behind stones and trees without your seeing them? We shall not meet your troops in the open veldt, don't you believe it; we shall go into Natal to meet you.

From the British perspective, this was an ominous prediction, because that is exactly what happened, at the cost of hundreds of British lives and at the cost of inflamed passions and the engendering of deeply felt resentments.

As matters moved towards what seemed like an inevitable clash, a meeting of Boers who were opposed to the annexation was held at Paardekraal on 8 December 1880 so that, stated Kruger, 'the people should then decide if a peaceful solution of the difficulties was possible'. However, as Kruger related, tension continued to escalate when, two days before it took place, the meeting was banned and those who were to take part in it were proclaimed rebels. Nevertheless, a large crowd of burghers met as arranged, and the meeting resolved that the government of the ZAR should resume office and should convene the *Volksraad*.

The business of government was entrusted to a triumvirate consisting of Kruger, as vice-president, Piet Joubert, as commandant general, and former president M.W. Pretorius. The triumvirate then proclaimed that the republic had been reinstated. The die was cast for confrontation.

Kruger described the plan of action as follows:

> In view of their very small number, in all about 7,000 men, it was necessary for the Boers to go to work with the greatest circumspection. The plan was to cut off all the villages in which the English had a garrison and to send the rest of the burghers to the Natal frontier, there to arrest the approaching enemy reinforcements.

The first armed clash at Potchefstroom, which was a minor affair, was followed soon afterwards by the disaster (from the British point of view) at Bronkhorstspruit on 20 December 1880. A column of British soldiers consisting of six officers and 258 men was marching from Lydenburg to reinforce the troops at Pretoria when it was accosted by a force of about 250 Boers. After a parley, the officer in command of the British force refused to halt or turn back. The Boers opened fire and, in a battle lasting just fifteen minutes, 156 British soldiers were killed or wounded, while the rest were taken prisoner. The Boers reported only two killed and five wounded.

Fisher drew attention to one of the ominous aspects of the battle when he wrote,

> It was at Bronkhorst Spruit that the extraordinary skill of these farmers with the rifle, to which the subsequent British reverses were all due, was first seen. The average of five wounds per man which is said to have been inflicted on the British soldiers in this skirmish was hitherto unheard of in civilized warfare.

During a much larger and more ruinous war less than twenty years later, Boer marksmanship, as unerring as ever, would inflict scores of thousands of casualties on British forces.

The Boers besieged the British garrisons while a mobile force advanced into Natal. There, after several defeats and reverses, the British experienced another disaster at Majuba Hill, where more than half of their force of 405 men was either killed or wounded. To compound the disaster, the British troops had occupied a supposedly unassailable hilltop, while the Boer fighters had to make their way up steep slopes, using whatever protection was available, covering each other with rifle fire and, from difficult positions, using their fine marksmanship to pick off British soldiers on the skyline. Astonishingly, the Boers had only two or three casualties.

Fitzpatrick, who was no great friend of the Boers, commented that it was impossible to detract from the performance of the Boers, because the British force seemed to be in such an unassailable position that a successful attack upon it seemed to be impossible. Fitzpatrick then went on to praise the Boers' fighting qualities, the leadership of their commander, the cleverness of the attack, and the bravery and audacity of the storming party. To rub salt into the considerable British wounds, the Boers were not professional soldiers, but farmers without specific military training; indeed, many of the Boer combatants were described as no more than farm boys.

During the discussions that led to the settlement of the dispute, Kruger, representing the Boers, and Sir Evelyn Wood, representing the British, had the following conversation (as reported by Kruger):

> [Wood asked], 'What were the two hundred men for, whom you were sending to the Biggarsberg?'
>
> [Kruger replied], 'We heard that you were marching there with 12,000 men.'
>
> 'And you sent your two hundred?'
>
> 'Yes, we had no more to send; but I have seen that they would have been sufficient for the purpose.'

In view of the size of the British defeats, and the massive disparities in the numbers of killed and wounded, Kruger's taunt that 200 Boers could defeat 12,000 British soldiers did not appear to be too far-fetched. However, it is likely that the Boers' military and diplomatic successes in this war gave them a distorted assessment of the forces and resources that the world's largest empire could muster and deploy, as well as its resolve, if it was determined to carry a fight through to a successful conclusion. In other words, the First Anglo-Boer War probably made the Boers over-confident that they could achieve the same result again. Their over-confidence and misreading of the situation could have contributed to taking them into the Second Anglo-Boer War, where there was a different result.

The dispute was settled with two conventions, in 1881 and 1884. These conventions restored independence to the ZAR, with one proviso, namely that the British exercised suzerainty over the republic. In effect, this meant that the British reserved the right to oversee and control its foreign affairs. This was an uneasy compromise because, as can be imagined, the question of suzerainty caused tensions and disagreements between the two parties. For instance, Kruger and his colleagues understood that suzerainty had been completely revoked in the second agreement, while the British claimed that this was not the case. Kruger wrote that he told the *Volksraad* after the 1884 agreement had been concluded that 'our independence had been obtained – that henceforward the Republic took her place as an equal with other independent powers, and that the suzerainty had ceased to exist'.

Significantly, in the treaties and elsewhere, the British insisted on using the name Transvaal, while the Boers insisted on using the name South African Republic.

After the British defeats and the revocation of the annexation, people in South Africa with British affiliations, and particularly those in the Transvaal, were angry at what they regarded as an abject and humiliating capitulation to the Boers. Heckford, who spent the war among those who were besieged in Pretoria, described the condition of one family, named Higgins, who had owned a farm before the war. Heckford wrote,

> They knew they were ruined. They tried to take it bravely, did take it bravely, but you saw that the knowledge struck home.

They had staked all on their faith in English trustworthiness. They had believed implicitly in the repeated asseverations of the Government that the Transvaal should remain British territory; they had broken utterly with the Boers, they had lost all their oxen and cows, all their sheep, all their crops, all but two of their horses, and they were destined henceforth to be subject to the men whom we, by our promises, had tempted them to turn from friendly neighbours into enemies.

Heckford continued,

Wherever you turned in that little camp [Pretoria] you saw faces, heard voices that told you of ruin; sometimes the thought of it was patiently borne, but the thought of the disgrace, which seemed to have been thrust on them, roused the anger of these men and women.

Humiliation, anger and a sense of disgrace – these emotions also played a role in stoking the passions that led to the outbreak of the Second Anglo-Boer War.

With independence restored, in the 1882 election for a state president, Kruger gained two-thirds of the votes. The principles that Kruger announced during his election campaign are worth repeating here, because of the insights that they provide into the mood, outlook, and situation in the ZAR at the time. Kruger listed these priorities:

God's Word should be my rule of conduct in politics and the foundation upon which the state must be established.
The promotion of agriculture;
the opening up of fresh resources of the country and their exploitation through the creation of new industries;
railway extension towards the sea;
restrictions on immigration…in order to prevent the Boer nationality from being stifled;
a friendly attitude towards England and a closer alliance of the South African states;
the maintenance of the authority of the Government towards the natives and the friendly treatment of obedient native races in their appointed districts;

the furtherance of all efforts which would bring the life of the people under the influence of the Gospel;

the advancement of instruction for the young.

Although peace with Britain had been secured, the Transvaal continued to be involved in hostilities with the natives. Kruger recorded,

At about the time when the election was held, the Republic became involved in a war with Mapoch in Secucuniland, in the east of the Republic… It lasted for nine months, and in order to bring it to a successful conclusion, at length it became necessary to place 4,000 burghers in the field.

Kruger placed the best construction on what must have been a frustrating and draining conflict for the Boers by stating that, through this war, the ZAR showed that it could handle all security matters itself. However, keeping about 4,000 men in the field for nine months would have been an enormous drain on the ZAR's resources, especially when it came so soon after the war against Britain. It was no wonder that Kruger tried to shorten the length of the engagement by visiting the scene several times to urge the burghers to try to end the conflict as quickly as possible.

During 1883, during a conflict between two Bechuana chiefs near the western parts of the ZAR, volunteers from both the ZAR and the Cape Colony became involved in the fighting on both sides. They did so because they were promised gifts of land in return for their services; when the conflict was over, these volunteers (mercenaries would be more appropriate) established two republics on the territories that had been granted to them. These short-lived republics, named Stellaland and Goshen, soon united. Almost predictably, with British citizens and Transvaal burghers involved, and with land acquisition the prize, the British and the ZAR disagreed over the matter. Another armed clash between the Boers and the British threatened when the ZAR annexed this territory. The British countered by sending an armed force to assert control over the territory, and then annexed it as part of the Protectorate of British Bechuanaland. Although the Transvaal did not actively contest the annexation, the confrontation increased the bad blood between the two parties.

The next armed clash was in 1885, when the Transvaal sent a commando against a chief on the western frontier named Massouw who, wrote Kruger, 'had voluntarily enrolled himself as a vassal of the Transvaal, but now refused to pay his taxes and assumed a very threatening attitude'. Once again, there was a heavy price to pay, not only in money and resources, but in lives; Kruger recorded that the Boers lost fourteen killed and about thirty wounded. The penalty for their opponents was heavy loss of life, followed by their tribe being broken up.

It is noteworthy that the Boer casualties were greater in some of the clashes with African tribesmen than they were when fighting against British regular forces. For instance, the Bechuana chief, Sechele, stated that when a Boer commando numbering four hundred men attacked his settlement in 1852, twenty-eight Boers were killed while, as seen above, fourteen Boers were killed and thirty wounded when a commando attacked Massouw's people in 1885. Proportionately, these casualties were much higher than those that the Boers suffered in clashes with the British at Bronkhorstspruit and Majuba. The reason was that by this time the African fighters were not only using firearms, and using them effectively, but were also fighting guerrilla-style while using natural cover, just as the Boers did. This can be seen in the following excerpt of Kruger's account of the clash with Secheli's forces:

> the Kaffirs were creeping up behind rocks and boulders, and I realized the danger to which my burghers would be exposed if they were not warned in time... The Kaffirs kept up a hot fire from every cave and gorge, but, after a sharp fight, the burghers succeeded in driving them from the mountain.

The days of Boers firing from behind cover, or from safe distances, into massed ranks of spear-wielding warriors were gone. The British commanders should have taken note of these developments.

18

Gold

Although the Boers had regained their independence, the outlook was far from bright. Kruger recorded that the state's financial situation was so poor that the bank would not advance any more credit. In fact, the financial situation was so poor that, if Fitzpatrick is correct, Kruger and his colleague, Nicolaas Smit, were unable to pay their hotel bill when they were in London in 1884 on an official mission to negotiate what became known as the London Convention. Kruger wrote that he had to exert himself to the utmost to encourage the burghers not to lose courage because, he said, help would surely come. Ironically, in view of the course of events, the help came from the discovery of what Kruger called 'the rich gold-fields of the Witwatersrand'. This event, stated Kruger, brought about such a complete revolution in the financial affairs of the ZAR that it 'entered upon a new phase with this discovery'. It was also the beginning of the end for the ZAR.

From 1873 onward, four gold-bearing sites were worked near the border with Mozambique, in the area that used to be called the Eastern Transvaal and is now within Mpumalanga Province. However, the early workings were comparatively small, as was the number of foreigners who were attracted by the prospects. Nor did the mining activities make a significant contribution to the state treasury. The discoveries on the Witwatersrand changed all that dramatically.

At this point, with the fortunes of the Transvaal about to change dramatically and irreversibly, as a stocktaking exercise, I am going to pause and review some of the major features and characteristics of the Boers and their state. I began by showing that the Boers' worldview was fundamentally Calvinist, of the seventeenth century variety. Some of the major features of this outlook were a fundamentalist belief that the Bible was 'the Word of God', a deep respect for those who pronounced and interpreted the Word to the congregation, and an adherence to democratic practice that was grounded in the autonomous decision-making of individual congregations. The Boers' fundamentalism was bolstered and nurtured not only by the fact that they were a homogenous, rural and self-sustaining society, but also by their (largely self-imposed) isolation from sources of intellectual change and development, such as humanism and the European Enlightenment. Conan Doyle aptly described the Boers as 'hard-bitten farmers with (their) ancient theology'.

The Boers' democratic tendency was accompanied by a strong predisposition to republicanism. As seen in the Great Trek, in the founding of independent republics, and in the strenuous efforts that the Boers made to keep their states autonomous, they wanted to be governed under their own constitutions and laws, and by their own, elected representatives.

The Boers also believed that they occupied a favoured and privileged position as Christian people who were surrounded and threatened by heathens. This conviction, together with the sense of European entitlement that found expression in colonialism with its expansionism, land seizure and disregard of the rights of indigenous inhabitants, underpinned their seemingly never-ending outward movements into new territories, whether already occupied or not. There was also a practical reason for the trek urge, namely that the large sizes of most families meant that each generation wanted to occupy new land to avoid a situation where existing settlements were increasingly sub-divided among family members until holdings became unviable. Expansionism and mobility via trekking were so common over such a long period that they became ways of life and developed into intrinsic aspects of Boer culture.

The Boers' belief that they were a favoured people, with its accompanying sense of cultural separateness and specificity, was fortified by the need for solidarity and joint action in the face of natural and human challenges. After they overcame hostile forces with vastly superior numbers and fearsome reputations, such as the Zulus and the Matabeles, the Boers' sense of being a favoured people strengthened and deepened. However, it is not certain that many Boers believed that they were, in fact, a chosen people with a divine mandate; it seems that this was a later development, when Afrikaner ideologues began to mythologise Boer experiences. This notwithstanding, the Boers did have a strong sense of group identity that manifested itself in the conviction that they needed to defend the integrity of their culture as well as their physical boundaries. The sense of group identity also included strongly held notions of racial purity.

In addition, the Boers' sense of communal solidarity was reinforced by the value that they attached to the practical aspects of their way of life, such as frugality, agrarian knowledge, bushcraft, horsemanship and marksmanship.

In the two Boer republics, the Boers were always a minority with a profound sense that the enemy was always at the gates, and always needed to be both subdued and kept at bay. For this reason, every burgher between eighteen and sixty years of age could be called upon to serve on a commando. The whole country was divided into districts, and each district was subdivided into wards, in each of which was an elected field cornet, who had military duties when a commando was called out. It was a society that was permanently prepared for armed conflict.

The Boer general, Christiaan De Wet, gave the following account of the requirements of the Commando Law in the Orange Free State:

> every burgher between the ages of sixteen and sixty must be prepared to fight for his country at any moment; (and that) if required for active service, he must provide himself with a riding-horse, saddle and bridle, with a rifle and thirty cartridges – or, if

he were unable to obtain a rifle, he must bring with him thirty bullets, thirty caps, and half a pound of powder – in addition he must be provisioned for eight days.

De Wet also provided an insight into the egalitarian functioning of a commando when he described how meat, a central item in a soldier's diet, was distributed among the men when they were on active duty. A commando member was specifically responsible for the job. He was named the *vleeschkorporaal* or meat corporal and had to be a man whose impartiality was above suspicion. To further ensure that there was no partiality or favouritism, the meat corporal would turn his back to the men while doling out the portions. As the men came up in turn, he would pick up the piece of meat which lay nearest to hand and, without looking round, give it to the man who was waiting behind him to receive it. Although this description of commando requirements and practices applies to the Orange Free State, the situation in the Transvaal would have been very similar.

With their strong sense of individualism and self-reliance, the Boers resisted state intrusion into their lives and especially disliked paying taxes. As it was on the American frontier, so it was in the Transvaal; in Turner's words (describing the situation in America) the tax-gatherer was viewed as a representative of oppression, and individual liberty was sometimes confused with absence of effective government. However, money had to be found somewhere to support a minimum of facilities and resources so that the state could function. These included institutions such as government and the administration of law and order, provisions for defence, providing and maintaining infrastructure such as public buildings and roads, and education. In addition, the constitution made provision for the state to provide subsidies for the upkeep of the church. However, even if the citizens had been favourably disposed to paying their taxes, and to paying generously, the state would almost certainly have struggled for income, because most Boers lived simple, agrarian lives, often engaged in exchange and barter rather than monetary transactions, and did not have much surplus.

Writing of his experiences during the 1870s, Aylward explained that one of the reasons why a relatively simple economy existed was the enormous expense of transporting goods to distant markets by ox wagon. He explained that because of the expense, 'it ought not to be reasonably expected that Transvaal farmers, for many years to come, should attempt to produce more than is likely to be required for immediate consumption in their own neighbourhoods'. After setting out the costs of hired transportation, Aylward explained that few Boer farmers would convey their own produce to the markets because of the length of time that they would be away from home, during which other affairs, some of them of greater importance, would be neglected.

Heckford depicted another aspect of the situation when she envisaged a typical farmer who, viewing his lands and possessions,

> thinks of all his possessions as things that he has perhaps won by toil, but with which, now that he has them, he is contented, looking for nothing beyond. His crops will realize a price which will enable him to live as he is living. If they fetch a higher price than usual, he can perhaps get a new wagon, or indulge in a half-bred English horse; or perhaps, if he be a very enterprising character, he may think he will some time take his children to Natal…

Aylward provided a similar insight when he described the house of the average Boer as being almost always the work of the owner's own hands, constructed without the assistance of skilled labour, and from materials found upon or near to the site.

This being the case, it was not surprising that the state finances were so impoverished during the mid-1880s that, as Kruger noted ruefully, the bank would not advance any further credit. This was not an isolated occurrence; for instance, even the most ardent supporters of Boer independence admitted that the ZAR was bankrupt when the British annexed it in 1877. Although matters improved during the period of the annexation, when the British took care of the public finances, by 1884 the ZAR was practically bankrupt again. This is how Fisher described the parlous situation:

It owed a sum of £396,000, which was just covered by the State lands, then valued at £400,000. Its revenue was £43,000 less than its expenditure...

In short, the state desperately needed money, and, in Kruger's words, the authorities wondered from which quarter help would come. When it did come, it came not in a trickle, but in a flood that at first buoyed up and then finally overwhelmed the ZAR.

Another factor that constrained the ZAR was the fact that between the mid-1870s and the mid-1880s, its boundaries were being firmly defined in almost every direction. It was if a fence was being constructed all around the Transvaal, bringing its period of expansionism to an end. To the east, the boundary with Portuguese-ruled Mozambique had been defined from the earliest days. To the south-west, diamond-rich Griqualand West, which the ZAR had tried to annex, became a British colony in 1873 and then part of the Cape Colony in 1880. North of Griqualand West, the British annexed the short-lived Republic of Stellaland and then attached it to the newly-created Bechuanaland Protectorate. This, together with the creation of the protectorate, defined all the western boundary of the Transvaal state and prevented further expansion in that quarter. To the south-east, the Transvaal's boundary was drawn when the British recognised the independence of Swaziland in 1881 (although it did have a short-lived stint as a protectorate of the ZAR from 1894 until the outbreak of the Anglo-Boer War in 1899). To the north in Matabeleland (later part of Rhodesia and then Zimbabwe), an agreement with Cecil Rhodes's agents in 1888 nullified an agreement that Lobengula, Moselikatse's son and successor, had made with the ZAR. Then, a few years later, after the Rhodes-dominated British South Africa Company conquered Lobengula and the Matabele kingdom, the region was completely closed to Boer expansion.

Although the Transvaal state was being constrained by a tightening noose of defined boundaries, many Boers still not only wanted to trek but managed to do so. Among the best known of these restless spirits are the *Dorsland* (Thirstland) Trekkers, who inspanned their wagons and, with families, servants, possessions and livestock, left the Transvaal to travel across present-day central and northern Botswana and northern Namibia. Some of them finally settled in present-day Namibia, while others pressed on to settle in south-western Angola.

Although it is called the *Dorsland* Trek, implying a single movement, this epic migration was undertaken by a number of parties between 1875 and 1877–8. The first trekkers suffered enormously from thirst, starvation, exhaustion, and fever. With so many different people in so many different parties being involved, and in the absence of reliable records, it is impossible to have an accurate tally of the number of casualties; nevertheless, there is no doubt that the suffering and death-rate were enormous. In some cases, entire family parties died, or only one or two people survived out of a party of ten or twelve persons. And yet, they pressed onward.

Why did they trek? Some of the trekkers were *Jerusalemgangers* (meaning those who are on the way to Jerusalem), who rejected the Dutch Reformed Church and seemed to believe that they could reach Utopia, perhaps Jerusalem itself, by trekking. However, these were a minority among the trekkers. More, probably, were trekking to escape from unacceptable political developments, such as the presidency of Thomas François Burghers, who was considered heretical by some Boers, as well to escape the annexation of the Transvaal by the hated British. Others trekked because that is what they did: with their wagons, servants, oxen and livestock, they moved across the great expanses of Africa...moving, always moving, and always looking towards the horizon, to see what lay beyond, and always believing that something better lay before them. For a while, they would settle down and would appear to be putting down roots; but the urge to trek was always present, and some or other impetus would get them moving again.

The *Dorslanders* were not the only Transvaal Boers with a trek-urge. As Kruger relates in his *Memoirs*, in 1891 he had to deal with the crisis of the Adendorff Trek. This is how Kruger described the matter:

The Adendorff trek had its origin in a concession which a certain Adendorff and Mr B. Foster, jun., had obtained in Banjailand and which they vainly endeavoured to sell to Cecil Rhodes. Rhodes declared that the concession was illegal, whereupon its owners resolved to trek to the territory which had been leased to them. The High Commissioner and Rhodes both opposed this trek, as they considered that it endangered the interests of the Chartered Company, and they asked me, in accordance with the Swaziland Convention, to forbid the trekkers to carry out their project. I immediately published a declaration against the trek and issued a proclamation in which the burghers throughout the country were strictly forbidden to take part in it.

Banjailand was the southern part of the territory that later became known as Rhodesia, and Rhodes considered that the territory was included in the agreement that his chartered company had made with Lobengula. However, Adendorff and Foster claimed that it lay outside the area that was covered by the agreement. The crisis was exacerbated by the fact that Adendorff and Foster gained the support of many Boers by casting the proposed trek in the mould of the *Voortrekkers*, with Rhodes and the company in the role of the hated, oppressive British.

The power and attraction of the trek myth among the Transvaal Boers is shown by the fact that the Banjailand issue was debated vigorously in the *Volksraad*, where Kruger was heavily criticised for preventing the trekkers from moving into the territory that they claimed. In addition, as Kruger said, his opposition to the trek caused several burghers to vote for his opponents. Fitzpatrick offered a somewhat different perspective when he wrote that the trek had been organised by Piet Joubert and his relatives, and Kruger stopped it when he was warned that if the trek proceeded, it could provoke war with Britain. Piet Joubert was not only Kruger's main opponent in a number of presidential elections but was the long-standing commandant-general. In addition, he had also acted as president from time to time. He would have been the second-most influential politician in the Transvaal and if it was true that he was behind the plan, then that would go a long way toward explaining why the Banjailand trek became such a contested issue. In fact, the 1893 election was close-run, with 7,911 votes for Kruger and 7,246 for Joubert. There were rumours that the election was rigged. Joubert appealed the result, but to no avail.

During 1893 and 1895, small parties of Boers left the Transvaal to follow the routes of the earlier *Dorsland* Trekkers. It is not known what motivated them. Perhaps these treks were reactions against the growing numbers of *uitlanders* in the Transvaal. Bryce suggested that these later treks were caused by dissatisfaction with factors such as 'the Hollander influence' (in other words, the number of Dutch citizens who were in senior positions in the state) as well as the maladministration of the Government. However, this opinion might have derived from Bryce's pro-British views.

At this point, I will return to the thread of financial affairs and the gold boom. Eybers described the situation and the dilemma well when he wrote that in 1885, very rich gold reefs were discovered in a territory 'which up to that time had been devoted only to pastoral and agricultural pursuits.' He continued by saying that because the burghers 'could not readily turn their hands to gold-mining', many thousands of foreigners streamed into the ZAR to work the mines. The Boers called these people the *uitlanders*, and it was they, as much as the riches from the gold, that changed the future of the ZAR.

Remarkable changes happened during the period from 1885 to the late 1890s, a period of less than fifteen years. Stanley described one aspect of the vast increase in investment, construction, and population during this time as follows:

> A photograph of Johannesburg taken in 1888 revealed a thin collection of galvanised iron structures, widely scattered over a roadless veld, while that of 1897 shows a mature city, compact, with an aspect of age, well furnished with churches, massive buildings, parks with trees over a hundred feet in height, rich villas and artistic mansions, etc. It was scarcely credible that in such a short period such a marvellous change had been wrought.

In short, the wealth that was extracted and produced was so immense, the energy and industry that was focused on the goldfields was so prodigious, and the expansion of population was so great, that within less than fifteen years a piece of bare veld was transformed into a flourishing and affluent city with facilities that rivalled those to be found anywhere in the world.

19

The *Uitlanders*

Amidst this explosion in wealth and infrastructural development, the critical political factor – the wedge that allowed Imperial ambitions to pry open the Transvaal door and finally to enter and take possession of the room – was the rapid growth in the number of *uitlanders*, all of whom were attracted by the opportunities that were created by the gold. For instance, whereas there were fewer than 12,000 *uitlanders* in the Transvaal in 1886, according to Fisher, in 1893 the population of Johannesburg was given as 40,000 and that of the rest of the Witwatersrand (the adjacent gold-bearing area) as 30,000; and in 1895 it was estimated that there were 60,000 white inhabitants in Johannesburg, and 45,000 in the rest of the Rand. In summary, during a period of less than ten years, the number of *uitlanders* increased nearly tenfold, from about 12,000 to about 105,000.

Although there were often wide variations in the estimates, one factor remained constant, namely that by the mid- to late-1890s, *uitlanders* outnumbered, or nearly outnumbered, the whole Boer population which, as seen earlier, by then probably numbered about 75,000 in total – that is. men, women and children. However, for the Boers the situation would have been exacerbated by the fact that most of the *uitlanders* were adult males, whereas of the total Boer population, probably less than one-fifth (or fewer than 15,000) were adult males. The worrying implication of these figures was that the franchise was restricted to adult males; therefore, if a significant proportion of male *uitlanders* qualified for, and were granted, citizenship and the franchise, they would outnumber and outvote the Boers. In Creswicke's words, 'These permanent visitors were scarcely appreciated by the Boers. They foresaw the alien transformed into the citizen, and objected to him.'

Fisher corroborated these facts when he wrote that what he termed 'an incomplete and badly classified census' in 1896 showed that there were 60,000 male *uitlanders* and 78,000 Boers. However, continued Fisher, while at least ninety-five per cent of male *uitlanders* were adults, the Boer burghers must have been considerably outnumbered. He supported this statement by showing that the number of voters in the presidential election of 1893 was 14,935, and in 1898 it was 18,612. In summary, whatever the actual figures were, it is certain that by the mid-1890s, *uitlanders* who could vote when enfranchised considerably outnumbered enfranchised Boers.

It must have been galling for Kruger and the Boers to reflect on the fact that it was these same, troubling *uitlanders* who, by developing and working the mines, produced such a rapid turnaround and improvement in the financial situation of the ZAR. As Kruger said in his *Memoirs*, whereas the state was almost bankrupt before the Witwatersrand gold fields were discovered, the opening up of the fields 'brought about a complete revolution in the financial aspect of the affairs of the Republic'. The improvement was so great that between 1884 and 1897, state revenue increased more than twentyfold, according to Fisher. The same writer continued by showing that in 1897, the state's revenue was made up of the following items: 'import duties, £1,276,319; railway dues, £737,366; prospecting licences, £427,230'. With his pro-Imperial views, Fisher was happy to draw attention to the fact that almost all of this revenue 'was derived from the various activities of the Outlanders'.

As early as 1875–6, President Burghers had proposed that a railway should be built to link the Transvaal with the east coast, to strengthen the Transvaal economically and to lessen the dependence on British colonies. However, nothing came of it, mainly because Burghers could not raise the necessary capital and financial support, and because of a lack of support at home. Less than twenty years later, the explosion of economic activity and wealth on the Witwatersrand changed the picture dramatically. The Cape Colony had begun a program of railway expansion during the 1870s and now, under an agreement with the Orange Free State, the Cape constructed a railway line through the OFS to the Transvaal. The first trains operated between Cape Town and Johannesburg in 1892.

However, the last eighty-odd kilometres between the Transvaal border and Johannesburg were only constructed after Kruger agreed to the Cape Government Railways having a two-year monopoly on traffic to and from the goldfields. Although Kruger and his colleagues did not want to make deals with British interests, and particularly not with Cecil Rhodes, who was then premier of the Cape Colony, they were forced to conclude this agreement because their east coast railway project was floundering because of a lack of capital. However, the agreement to operate the Cape railway line renewed investor confidence, and by the time the agreement ended in 1894, the Transvaal–Mozambique line was operational. A tariff war then began, with Rhodes and his government trying to grab as much traffic as possible for the Cape line, and Kruger trying to divert as much traffic as possible to the Mozambique line.

The railway question was a thorny one for Kruger and his *Raad*. As Kruger records in his *Memoirs*, when he returned from a tour of Europe in 1884 with a railway concession agreement concluded but not financed, the *Volksraad* at first refused to ratify the concession because it feared that it would entail raising taxes. In 1887 Kruger failed to conclude an agreement of closer cooperation with the Orange Free State partly because, as Kruger said, he insisted that the Orange Free State should not permit a railway to be built through its territory. He explained that he was opposed to a closer connection with the British South African states so long as the independence of the Transvaal was not secured by having a railway of its own. However, even the Orange Free State, which was usually a staunch ally of the

ZAR, wanted to facilitate a rail link between Johannesburg and the Cape – thus cooperating with a British colony – because it wanted to have a share in the wealth that was being generated by the gold mines.

Despite their misgivings, Kruger and his *Raad* had to agree to allow the Cape rail line to extend from the Transvaal border to Johannesburg. Kruger says nothing about this in his *Memoirs*, probably because he was embarrassed at having to make a concession to interests that he hated and despised, namely Rhodes and British capitalists. A further factor in making the concession was that Kruger and his government came under pressure from the Afrikaner Bond political party in the Cape. Although the Afrikaner Bond usually supported its fellow-Afrikaners in the Transvaal, on this occasion, for commercial reasons the Bond favoured the completion of the railway.

The next act in the drama almost ended in war. In the tariff competition that followed the opening of the Johannesburg–Delagoa Bay railway line, the Transvaal government raised tariffs on the portion of the Cape line that was within their territory, to encourage use of the Delagoa Bay line. In response, the Cape Government Railways lowered tariffs on the portion of their line from the northern border of the Orange Free State southwards, and transported goods from the Transvaal border to Johannesburg in ox wagons. Kruger responded by closing the drifts, or river fords, to all traffic. (There were no road bridges over the Vaal River.) This move raised such a storm of protest, and such a furious citing of international agreements and points of law, that the British government sent an ultimatum to the ZAR. The latter backed down and opened the drifts to traffic. In time, presumably the tariffs on the Transvaal portion of the Cape railway line were normalised.

The drifts crisis was a precursor to the Jameson Raid, which was a central factor in the escalation of the tensions that eventually led to the outbreak of war in 1899.

The last major rail link with the Transvaal was completed when the line between Johannesburg and Durban opened in late 1895. After all the sound and fury that surrounded the early years of the operation of the Cape line, there is no indication that there was any fuss about the Natal line.

The opening of the Witwatersrand mines, the flood of *uitlanders*, and the increased international tensions, all coincided with a period during which the traditional lifestyle of many Boers was under pressure. The main reason was that because of the stabilising of the geographical boundaries of the Transvaal, no new lands could be opened for expansion, while at the same time many Boer farms had been so extensively subdivided that they were no longer viable economic units. Attempts to squeeze as much productivity as possible out of the over-populated, too-small units degraded the soil, and thus lowered productivity. In addition, after the *rinderpest* epidemic of 1896 destroyed huge numbers of animals, many farmers were too poor to restock their herds and to afford the improvements that were necessary, such as constructing fencing. Driven into bankruptcy, they had to leave the land, and, with few appropriate skills and little education, they had to try to make their livings in the towns and cities, where they felt themselves to be foreigners in their own land. Because of these factors, a poor white problem was developing in the Transvaal. These poor whites, who were almost all Boers, felt deprived and marginalised in their own country. It was an explosive situation.

Ironically, the growing poor white problem coincided with a period during which the state's financial situation steadily improved. Creswicke produced figures that showed how quickly, and by how much, the share of wealth had changed in the Transvaal after the opening of the Witwatersrand gold mines. (The date to which these figures apply is not stated, but it appears to be the late 1890s.) In summary, although the Boers still owned twice as much land as the *uitlanders*, the *uitlander*-owned land was worth twice as much as that owned by the Boers. Creswicke stated that the figures were given by 'Mr. Campbell, late Vice-President of the Chamber of Mines, Johannesburg', who based his conclusions on data in the Government

Dues Office at Pretoria. However, because (quote) 'all land occupied for mining or town sites is excluded', the value of foreign-owned land overall would have been much higher.

	Ownership of land	Value of land
Boers	65%	33%
British	35%	67%

It is not difficult to imagine that tensions between Boers and *uitlanders* would be increasing, fuelled by factors such as the growing poor white problem; the fact that many Boers no longer owned land or occupied productive units; the growing rural poverty caused in part by the *rinderpest*; the huge and growing wealth gap between the two groups; and, as we will see, the use of the *uitlanders* as a wedge for Imperial interests. To add to the tensions, most of the *uitlanders* were British, and were thus associated with the hated power from whose control the Boers had trekked, and against whose forces they had fought more than once.

Another factor that must have been causing tensions in Boer society was the increasing inequality. Until the opening of the Witwatersrand mines, Boer society was relatively egalitarian in terms of income, possessions and status: that is, there were few extremes of wealth and poverty, and most people had similar lifestyles, with similar skills, education, occupations and possessions. However, as we have seen, the gold changed the situation, and changed it quickly.

The buildings that were erected in Church Square in the centre of old Pretoria are visual reminders of the newly affluent condition of the state. The first, and one of the grandest, was the *Ou Raadsaal*, or Old Parliament Building, which was completed during 1890. This three-storey building in the impressive Beaux Arts style was designed by the ZAR's first government engineer and architect, a Dutchman named Sytze Wopka Wierda, who was recruited from Amsterdam, where he was well respected. Wierda designed the Amsterdam Railway Station, among others. The fact that that the ZAR was able to attract a man

The Raadsaal (Government) Building in Church Square, Pretoria (1890) – one of many facilities built by income from the gold mines.

with such a good reputation shows that both the remuneration offered, and the challenges, were appealing.

The building, which was the first to bear the ZAR's coat of arms, also paraded the state's new-found wealth and assertiveness by having telephones installed in 1892 and electric lighting in 1896. Kruger took a close personal interest in the design and construction of the building and arranged for a third floor to be added so that it would be higher than the neighbouring hotel.

Wierda also designed the equally impressive Palace of Justice on Church Square, which was opened in 1896. All in all, as head of the state's Department of Public Works, Wierda oversaw more than one hundred and twenty construction projects between 1887 and 1899. Many of these were road bridges, which were the first ever constructed in the Transvaal. Until then, travellers faced delays from swollen rivers and unreliable river crossings (drifts). Other projects included military buildings such as the forts around Pretoria and Johannesburg, and various official buildings such as courthouses, post offices, jails and police stations. This flurry of construction activity within the comparatively short period of twelve years testified to the vastly increased income of the state treasury after the Witwatersrand gold mines opened.

As always, new wealth was accompanied by new problems and new temptations. Amongst the litany of complaints made by the *uitlanders* against Kruger and his government, was that they were financially corrupt. Bryce wrote that

> the old Boer virtues were giving way under new temptations. The new *Volksraad* (as is believed all over South Africa) became corrupt, though of course there have been always pure and upright men among its members. The Civil Service was not above suspicion.

Stanley, always a jingoist, wrote that the *uitlanders* complained about 'the bakshish-begging *Raad*, the bribe-taking Ministry…'

Fisher claimed that Kruger told the *Volksraad* that he did not see why members should not accept gifts. In fact, wrote Fisher, to the Boers, national prosperity meant the provision of a much bigger pie, into which everyone could dig their fingers. He then continued to list some of the matters that scandalised the *uitlanders*; these included public officials taking bribes of hundreds of pounds from a contractor for the draining of Johannesburg. There were similar revelations about the sale of sites on public land for £8,000 each, when they should have realised £37,000 each. Fisher said that the difference mainly went into the pockets of *Volksraad* members. He claimed that a member of the Executive benefited from the dynamite monopoly by £10,000 per year. Fisher further maintained that

> A long list could be made of the pickings which President Kruger and his relations have had out of the State, with the tacit and sometimes open support of the *Volksraad*, who held it a crime to muzzle the ox that trod out their corn.

If reports were correct, then even Kruger was also involved in fraud and corruption. Fitzpatrick reported a case in which Kruger's son-in-law, Frikkie Eloff, was involved in a dubious property transaction. In this case, Eloff prospered when Kruger went against a decision of the

Volksraad and, by buying the land for the state, enabled Eloff to pocket £25,000.

These allegations were made by authors who were unashamedly and aggressively pro-British, so they should be viewed with some caution. Their greatest significance lies in the fact that they were widely circulated and believed in anti-ZAR circles and were among the many accusations that the *uitlanders* directed at the government. However, far more acute than dissatisfaction with alleged corruption, was the *uitlanders'* dissatisfaction with the many monopolies that were maintained by the state and which, claimed the *uitlanders*, unnecessarily raised the cost of living and the cost of doing business. Chief among these was the dynamite monopoly which kept the price artificially high; and dynamite was an essential commodity for the mining industry.

By the mid-1890s, the relationship between the government and the *uitlanders* was severely tainted by dislike and suspicion. For instance, Kruger complained that the *uitlanders* 'were always on the watch to invent grievances against the President and the Government'. Basically, the government felt that the *uitlanders* were there for no other purpose than to make money – which they were doing very successfully – and that their loyalties lay with their mother country and not with the ZAR. The *uitlanders'* counter accusation was that the government was milking the products of their energy, labour, and capital for as much as it could without actually killing the goose that was laying the golden egg, for the sole purpose of benefiting the state and its accredited citizens, namely the Boers of the Transvaal. It was a condition of mutual dependence that irritated both parties.

Stanley noted that the *uitlanders* were 'labouring under a sense of wrong, and disposed to be querulous and recriminatory'. (This was during the late 1890s, after the Jameson Raid and not long before war was declared.) He further noted that, after complaining that they had been neglected and betrayed by the British government which, the *uitlanders* said, should have looked after their interests in terms of the 1884 convention,

They then proceeded to dilate upon Boer oppression, Boer corruption, the cant and hypocrisy of President Kruger, the bakshish-begging *Raad*, the bribe-taking Ministry, the specious way in which promises were made, and, when their trust was won, the heartless way in which these same promises were broken.

But there was more, wrote Stanley: the *uitlanders* then continued by complaining about

high wages, extortionate freight charges, the exactions levied upon every necessity of their industry, the exorbitant price for coal, and imposts on food designed expressly to pamper the burgher at the expense of the miner.

However, all other causes of dissatisfaction paled next to the franchise issue. To put it simply, many *uitlanders* began to demand that, after a qualifying period, they should be allowed to become citizens and to exercise the franchise so that they could be directly involved in the political decisions that affected their lives and businesses. The fire of their dissatisfaction was stoked by British interests, such as capitalists who were eyeing greater control over the gold wealth, and by the British government itself, which had the dual aim of unifying all Southern Africa under British control and, by so doing, controlling all its wealth. There was a close correspondence between the interests of the British government and the interests of the capitalists. For instance, all the British-based members of the board of the British South Africa Company were politically and socially influential members of the British ruling class.

As time went by, the franchise issue became the instrument that pro-British, capitalistic interests wielded to force the government of the ZAR either to back down or to go to war. It was one of the ostensible issues that provoked the Jameson Raid, which followed hard on the heels of the Drifts Crisis. In fact, with the raid taking place only two months after the Drifts Crisis had been resolved, it is not difficult to suppose that the raid was an expression of Rhodes's growing frustration with what he regarded as Kruger's obdurate obstructionism.

20

The Jameson Raid and War

The Jameson Raid took place at a time when *uitlander* dissatisfaction had reached the point where there was serious talk of staging an armed uprising to overthrow the government. To support their plans, the plotters, who had established a Reform Committee, surreptitiously imported arms and ammunition into Johannesburg. Cecil Rhodes, the premier of the Cape Colony, and several of his capitalist colleagues were not only kept informed of developments – it was helpful that Rhodes' brother was a member of the Reform Committee – but supported and encouraged the plot. They not only fanned the fire, but also added fuel whenever possible.

During December 1895, which was less than two months after the Drifts Crisis ended, Rhodes instructed Leander Starr Jameson to assemble an armed force on the Transvaal's western border in what was then known as Bechuanaland. Jameson was the administrator of Mashonaland for Rhodes's Chartered Company, and most of the five hundred men under his command were from the Mashonaland force. The aim was to invade the Transvaal and trigger an armed uprising in Johannesburg. This is how Creswicke describes the events:

> Arms and ammunition were purchased, and these, concealed as gold-mining impedimenta, were smuggled into the country. Messrs. Leonard and Phillips, two prominent Reformers, consulted Mr. Rhodes as to future affairs, but Mr. Rhodes was in the awkward position of acting at one and the same time as Managing Director of the Consolidated Gold Fields in the Transvaal, Prime Minister of the Colony, and Managing Director

of the Chartered Company, and consequently was a little vague in his propositions. After some conversation, he decided that he would, at his own expense, keep Dr. Jameson and his troops on the frontier 'as a moral support.'

After dithering and confusion, either Rhodes or Jameson, or both, became impatient and the force crossed the border. The government knew exactly what was happening and a Boer force intercepted the raiders. After an exchange of fire and some casualties, the invaders surrendered. To compound the failure of the plot, the hoped-for uprising in Johannesburg did not take place. Instead, leading members of the Reform Committee were arrested and charged with high treason. Those who were regarded as ringleaders received severe sentences, while the majority escaped with high fines. When a second trial of the Reform Committee was held during late April, the leaders were condemned to death; however, the punishments were commuted to fines and imprisonment, as a gesture of magnanimity on the part of President Kruger and his government. By mid-June, Kruger released the last seven Reform Committee members after each paid a big fine.

Mark Twain visited the Transvaal soon after the raid took place and, only partly tongue in cheek, he summarised the events as follows:

> After a couple of years of judicious plotting, Mr. Rhodes had his reward; the revolutionary kettle was briskly boiling in Johannesburg, and the *Uitlander* leaders were backing their appeals to the government – now hardened into demands – by threats of force and bloodshed. By the middle of December, 1895, the explosion seemed imminent. Mr. Rhodes was diligently helping, from his distant post in Cape Town. He was helping to procure arms for Johannesburg; he was also arranging to have Jameson break over the border and come to Johannesburg with 600 mounted men at his back. Jameson – as per instructions from Rhodes, perhaps – wanted a letter from the Reformers requesting him to come to their aid. It was a good idea. It would throw a considerable share of the responsibility of his invasion upon the Reformers. He got the letter – that famous one urging him to fly to the rescue of the women and children. He got it two

months before he flew. The Reformers seem to have thought it over and concluded that they had not done wisely; for the next day after giving Jameson the implicating document they wanted to withdraw it and leave the women and children in danger; but they were told that it was too late.

The members of the invading force were handed over to the British government for trial and were taken to London as prisoners. Jameson was sentenced to fifteen months in prison and the British South Africa Company paid almost £1 million to the Transvaal government as compensation. From the British point of view – from the jingoist point of view, anyway – about the only immediate, positive result of the raid was that British public opinion was roused against Germany when the Kaiser sent a telegram to Kruger and the ZAR government, congratulating them on their success in defeating the plot.

If the Jameson Raid and its sequel had been a boxing contest, Kruger and his government would have won it with a knockout during the first twenty seconds.

First, they completely defeated and crushed both the raiders and the Reform Committee plotters with hardly a casualty on their side.

Second, the Afrikaner Bond in the Cape, which only a few months earlier had criticised the Transvaal during the drifts crisis, broke its alliance with Rhodes and moved towards a pro-Boer position.

Third, the Orange Free State also re-evaluated its position and moved much closer to its fellow Boers in the Transvaal.

Fourth, Kruger and his government gained international sympathy as the wronged party in the incident.

Fifth, Kruger was admired for his magnanimous and lenient treatment of the raiders and plotters.

Sixth, Rhodes had to resign as premier of the Cape Colony, while he and his fellow conspirator, Alfred Beit, had to resign their places on the board of the British South Africa Company.

Seventh, Kruger won the next presidential election, which he might well have lost to Joubert if it had not been for the Raid.

Another consequence of the affair was that the British Colonial Secretary, Joseph Chamberlain, was implicated in the raid and offered to resign, but was retained in his position.

However, for Kruger and the Boers, an ominous aspect of the raid was the fact that, even although Jameson was convicted and imprisoned, he was wildly popular in Britain. It was clear that Jameson's anti-Boer actions decisively trumped the fact that, acting on behalf of commercial interests, he had led an invasion of a country with which Britain was not at war. In fact, Jameson's reckless and futile actions did not blight his reputation, and he went on to have a successful political career in the Cape after the Anglo-Boer War.

The raid galvanised the Transvaal government into preparing for war. It began to import modern arms and armaments and built forts around Johannesburg and Pretoria. In addition, the raid inflamed anti-British sentiment among Boers in both the Transvaal and the Orange Free State. Reitz expressed the feelings of many Boers when he wrote that

> Mr. Rhodes, with that treacherous duplicity which is an enduring characteristic of British policy in South Africa, co-operated publicly, and in the closest relationship, with the Colonial Africanders [that is, South Africans with British sympathies], while he was secretly fomenting a conspiracy with Jingoism against the Cape Africanders and the South African Republics.

The reference to Cape Africanders alludes to the fact that the Afrikaner Bond in the Cape Colony, which had been in alliance with Rhodes, split with him in disgust at his role in the raid. They and many others felt that Rhodes had betrayed them, by pretending to do one thing, namely to be seeking a peaceful and equitable outcome to the dispute, while secretly planning the opposite.

Kruger said in his *Memoirs* that the raid was primarily an initiative by Rhodes to gain territory and enrich himself. He stated that

> [Rhodes] forthwith explored Matabeleland in all directions in search of gold, but with poor results. So he decided to grab the rich gold-fields of the South African Republic, the high road to

which was the possession of South Africa itself. History knows the successful outcome of this base design!

In addition, Kruger stated that although Chamberlain claimed that he was not implicated in the raid, in fact he was fully informed at all stages. Furthermore, said Kruger, although Rhodes initially denied it, he used his position as premier of the Cape to facilitate the raid. Most historians would agree with Kruger's version of the motives and events.

Kruger was dismissive of the intentions and abilities of the members of the Reform Committee, whom he regarded as no more than pawns for Imperial interests. He said that the members surrendered without resistance because

> with the exception of Colonel Rhodes and perhaps one or two more, there was not one among the conspirators but would have taken to his heels as soon as the first shot was fired. They had wooed and organised rebellion only in the hope that England would pull the chestnuts out of the fire for them.

He also confirmed that the raid galvanised his government into making military preparations, mainly by exposing the fact that there were insufficient rifles and stocks of ammunition to arm the burgher forces properly. The government took steps to rectify the situation, with the result that the commando members were well equipped and well supplied when war broke out.

Writing from exile after 1902, when his country had been defeated, Kruger summed up the situation like this:

> And so the attempt upon the independence of the Republic failed. But now Mr. Chamberlain was to set to work to try whether he could not be more successful. With his assistance, Jameson's Raid was to be replaced by a gigantic British Raid.

Although he was writing from a pro-British position, Creswicke had to admit that the raid was a complicated riddle, the intentions of which had defied all the Oedipuses of the century. He listed a number of the apparently inexplicable aspects of the incident as follows:

Did Mr. Rhodes engage in the plot for the sake of financial gain? Did he do so out of sympathy for the 'cause,' or did he attempt a magnificent political coup? And lastly – Did that unhappy scapegoat, the gallant Jameson, launch himself on the wild mistaken escapade to rescue his fellow-countrymen from oppression, to serve his private ends financial or political, or from the sheer spirit of adventure which, in some degree, animates every British heart? Who shall say?

It is significant that, even as he admitted that the raid was an ill-conceived disaster, Creswicke tried to put lipstick on the pig by referring to the gallant Jameson, the oppression under which his countrymen were suffering in Johannesburg, and the British spirit of adventure. The pro-war jingoes would seize upon these themes as they began to develop the momentum towards a final reckoning with the Transvaal Boers.

The raid was such a hare-brained, ill-conceived and risky adventure that it seems almost inconceivable that anybody, particularly experienced and apparently well-informed politicians like Rhodes and Chamberlain, should have contemplated it, let alone actually have launched it. On the other hand, perhaps one could entertain the idea that the raid was intended to fail so that the whole episode would concentrate and inflame British public opinion and so prepare the way for the war that followed. A conspiracy theory such as this could be just as valid as many of the other speculations about this event.

The way Jameson was received by the British public (that is, as a hero and a gallant adventurer) must have convinced Joseph Chamberlain and his anti-Boer, pro-intervention colleagues that the public could easily be manipulated into anti-Boer fervour. That being the case, having tried an illegitimate venture and failed, the time had come to whip up support for a legitimate venture that had a much better chance of success, namely war against the South African Republic.

There was need for haste and decisive action because plans for a union of Southern African states under British control were losing traction. The Afrikaner Bond had split with Rhodes and was more sceptical than ever of British intentions; in their disgust at the raid, many Afrikaners in the Cape and Natal had become disillusioned and had become more sympathetic toward the Boers of the Transvaal and the Orange Free State; and the latter two states had moved closer to each other by signing a treaty of mutual defence and support. Ominously for British plans for a union of states, the Transvaal and the Orange Free State began to discuss 'matters that might lead to federation as well as suggestions for the assimilation of the laws of the two Republics' (in Kruger's words). In addition, the voters in the Transvaal had shown their support for policies that toughened the ZAR's position on British and *uitlander* plans by voting overwhelmingly for Kruger in the Transvaal presidential election. Kruger said of the election result that it 'came as a surprise to friends and enemies alike; for, although my re-election was certain, no one suspected that I would obtain such an overwhelming majority'. With the defeated candidate, Piet Joubert, regarded as being more inclined to amelioration and compromise, the election result showed that Boer attitudes towards Britain and the *uitlanders* were hardening.

With escalating crises and war being planned by influential politicians, Kruger described the ensuing events as follows:

> Meanwhile Mr. Chamberlain had found the man he wanted for his dealings with the South African Republic. In 1897, Sir Alfred Milner was appointed Governor of Cape Colony and High Commissioner for South Africa... There is no doubt that Mr. Chamberlain appointed Sir Alfred Milner only with a view of driving matters in South Africa to extremes.

Kruger's opinion was that 'Lord Milner is the typical Jingo, autocratic beyond endurance and filled with contempt for all that is not English.'

The central issue that the pro-war forces used to further their cause was the question of the franchise for the *uitlanders*. It was an issue on which the two parties were almost certainly never going to reach agreement, because Kruger and his government knew that the likely result of granting the franchise to the *uitlanders* would be that the Boers would lose power in their own land. Conan Doyle related a story which, although probably apocryphal, captured the essence of the issue:

> One who remonstrated [with Kruger] was led outside the State buildings by the President, who pointed up at the national flag. 'You see that flag?' said he, 'If I grant the franchise, I may as well pull it down.'

It was ironical that British politicians and their supporters were demanding ever more generous franchise conditions for the *uitlanders* when, in fact, only a relatively small proportion of adult males (probably less than thirty per cent) had the franchise in Britain. However, ironies and inconsistencies have never deterred politicians when they are in hot pursuit of a profitable goal and when they sense that they have the opposition on the back foot.

For a flavour of the spectrum of arguments that were used by the pro-war parties, we can look at what Conan Doyle wrote:

> A handful of people [that is, the Boers] by the right of conquest take possession of an enormous country over which they are dotted at such intervals that it is their boast that one farmhouse cannot see the smoke of another, and yet, though their numbers are so disproportionate to the area which they cover, they refuse to admit any other people upon equal terms, but claim to be a privileged class who shall dominate the newcomers completely. They are outnumbered in their own land by immigrants who are far more highly educated and progressive, and yet they hold them down in a way which exists nowhere else upon earth. What is their right? The right of conquest. Then the same right may be justly invoked to reverse so intolerable a situation.

In summary, the pillars on which the argument rested were: 1. the country was under-utilised; 2. the *uitlanders* were more numerous and more enterprising than the Boers, but were denied their rights; 3. because the Boers claimed the land as theirs by right of conquest, another party (that is, the British) could do the same if they went to war and defeated the Boers.

Conan Doyle also repeated other criticisms that were common in the pro-war elements of the British press, when he wrote about Kruger that,

> Those were his great days, the days when he hardened his heart against their [the *uitlanders*'] appeals for justice and looked beyond his own borders to his kinsmen in the hope of a South Africa which should be all his own.

Here, Conan Doyle aired two arguments that were commonly used against Kruger: 1. that he was denying justice and rights to the *uitlanders*, and 2. that he wanted to unite all South Africa under Afrikaner control. In fact, the latter claim was true; it was opposed by British and capitalist interests because it conflicted with the British desire to do the same, to further their own Imperial interests.

For Conan Doyle, the Boer fighters were 'brave honest farmers, but standing unconsciously for medievalism and corruption', who should be contrasted with 'our rough-tongued Tommies' (that is, British soldiers) who, in his opinion, 'stood for civilisation, progress, and equal rights for all men'. Like many British commentators, Conan Doyle portrayed the conflict as a clash of values, in which the British were on the side of enlightenment and modernity.

During the year before the war began, Stanley provided an even longer list of negative Boer qualities when he wrote that

> the real Kruger is a Boer Machiavelli, astute and bigoted, obstinate as a mule, and remarkably opinionated, vain and puffed up with the power conferred on him, vindictive, covetous and always a Boer, which means a narrow-minded and obtuse provincial of the illiterate type.

Clearly, anyone who removed such a person from his position of power would be doing the world a great favour! And clearly Stanley, who formed this impression while he was making a whistle-stop tour of the region by rail during his first and only visit to Southern Africa, was well qualified to pass judgement.

As tensions mounted, President Steyn of the Orange Free State invited Milner and Kruger to attend a conference in Bloemfontein. Although Kruger made concessions, the conference broke down, with Milner demanding full equality for British citizens resident in the Transvaal. Between June and early October 1899, communiqués passed between the parties, but with no agreement in sight, troops were mobilised on both sides, and war was inevitable. It was merely a question of when it would be declared. Kruger got in ahead of Chamberlain by issuing his ultimatum first.

Although the Jameson Raid was a disaster and a complete failure, it paved the way for war by making it clear to the jingoist party in British politics that the British public was not opposed to the use of force against the ZAR. Also, by consolidating pro-Boer alliances and support, the raid closed the avenues along which the imperialistic aims of a united South Africa under the British flag could be pursued. In summary, the Jameson Raid convinced the anti-Boer party in British politics that they would have to achieve their aims by military means, and that they should do so quickly. The pro-war party then chose the franchise as their main wedge against Kruger and his government, firstly because it was already one of the *uitlanders'* main grievances and secondly because they knew that Kruger would never yield on the issue beyond the point at which he felt that Boer votes would be surpassed by the *uitlanders'* votes. Thirdly, the issue allowed for ever-escalating demands to be made: if Kruger made concessions, as in fact happened, then more demands could be made, claiming the concessions were insufficient.

On the Boer side, Kruger's assessment that a war was inevitable was a correct reading of the situation. He and his government decided to hasten events because they knew that the British were relatively unprepared; in fact, during the first months of the war, the Boers probably had more men in the field than did the British. In addition, it is probable that the Boers were over-confident because of their successes during the First Anglo-Boer War and against Jameson's force. Writing during 1897, Mark Twain provided this sardonic account of the military imbalance between the two parties:

> Let us now examine history, and see what it teaches. In the 4 battles fought in 1881 and the two fought by Jameson, the British loss in killed, wounded, and prisoners, was substantially 1,300 men; the Boer loss, as far as is ascertainable, was about 30 men. These figures show that there was a defect somewhere. It was not in the absence of courage. I think it lay in the absence of discretion. The Briton should have done one thing or the other: discarded British methods and fought the Boer with Boer methods, or augmented his own force until – using British methods – it should be large enough to equalise results with the Boer. To retain the British method requires certain things, determinable by arithmetic. If, for argument's sake, we allow that the aggregate of 1,716 British soldiers engaged in the four early battles was opposed by the same aggregate of Boers, we have this result: the British loss of 700 and the Boer loss of 23 argues that in order to equalise results in future battles you must make the British force thirty times as strong as the Boer force.

It is likely that the Boers thought that by achieving quick victories and relying on their superior marksmanship and use of terrain, as in the earlier war, they would force a rethink and re-evaluation of the situation on the part of the British politicians, resulting in a negotiated compromise. However, during the first war, there was no pro-war party in Britain. On that occasion, the politicians were caught off guard. Now, in this second war, there was a strong pro-war party that had not only long been preparing for the conflict but was able to mobilise public opinion to support the war as a patriotic cause. Nor, probably, did the Boers anticipate that the British would mobilise all their resources for the conflict, and that unconditional surrender (and not a negotiated settlement, as in the past) would be the aim.

War broke out on 11 October 1899. The Anglo-Boer War, also

called the South African War, has been written about so often, and from so many angles and perspectives, that there is nothing new that I can say about it. However, I will write about the last stages of the war, because what happened then strongly influenced South Africa for the next ninety-odd years.

After the British forces captured the two Boer capital cities and President Kruger retreated into exile, by mid-1900 (that is, about nine months after the war began) it looked as if the war was almost at an end. The Boer forces were in disarray and thousands of Boer fighters had been captured. In addition, made despondent by the confusion and uncertainty, many had given up the struggle and had laid down their arms and returned home.[12] However, the surviving Boer fighters then began a guerrilla campaign that lasted for another eighteen months.

This phase of the war vastly increased the Boers' bitterness, resentment and hatred for the British. Almost all wars embitter and poison the relationship between the parties; however, the Second Anglo-Boer War was distinguished as being among those which left a deeply etched legacy of bitterness and resentment that lasted for almost a century. Doyle described the last phase of the war as follows:

> as the months went on and the struggle still continued, the war assumed a harsher aspect. Every farmhouse represented a possible fort, and a probable depot for the enemy. The extreme measure of burning them down was only carried out after a definite offence… Thus, on humanitarian grounds there were strong arguments against this policy of destruction being pushed too far, and the political reasons were even stronger, since a homeless man is necessarily the last man to settle down, and a burned-out family the last to become contented British citizens.

In summary, to counter the guerrilla tactics, the British commanders began to burn homesteads and destroy livestock and crops. The women and children were interned in camps.

In the camps, women and children died in their tens of thousands, from malnutrition, disease and unsanitary conditions, among other causes. But why did it happen? Was it deliberate policy or was it merely neglect? If it was neglect, then it was neglect on a massive scale, because it is estimated that about 26,000 women and children died during a period of about eighteen months. To put that figure into context, about one quarter of all women and children in the two Boer republics died in the camps. Of all the many, contested, conflict-ridden aspects of the war, the suffering and death of so many women and children in the concentration camps probably caused the most bitterness, resentment and hatred. Even today, more than a century after the war, many Afrikaners still remember the camps and speak about them with sadness, bitterness and resentment.

Here, it should be said that although the focus has almost solely been on the suffering and deaths of Boer women and children, the fate of many black people has been little mentioned. It is claimed that a similar number of black prisoners also died in the concentration camps. These black prisoners would have been farm hands, house servants, and *agterryers* (literally those who rode behind) who supported and assisted the commando members.

On a personal note, when I was a boy, I sometimes heard Afrikaners accusing the British of putting ground glass into the food that they served in the camps, to ensure that the prisoners not only died, but did so slowly and painfully. (I have read that, for many years, some of the ground glass was on display in the Anglo-Boer War Museum in Bloemfontein.) Although serious writers and researchers only mention the ground glass in the context of myths about the war, the fact that I heard the claim more than a few times from Afrikaners who believed it and resented it, is another indication of just how deep was the animosity that was caused by the camps.

Not surprisingly, Boer accounts of the war, and particularly of the guerrilla phase, are less restrained than Conan Doyle's account. Here, by a Boer fighter, is an account of women and children fleeing in terror from indiscriminate British shelling:

Many waggons of Boer families, fleeing for their lives, were pushing along the sides of the long mounds, and the enemy's bombs burst in their midst more than once – perhaps accidentally, perhaps because they knew that 'the Boer nation must be swept off the face of the earth.' The women seemed to be in a panic. From all sides families came in carts and waggons – long rows of vehicles filled with poor, terror-stricken women and children; large herds of cattle were driven along by the *Kaffir* servants, but many of them fell into the enemy's hands.

The author went on to say, 'It was a cruel sight, and it moved us strangely.'

The author also wrote about an assault on a Boer home by British soldiers, who first asked for money and then, while searching the house, found some dynamite which the farmer used for blasting wells. This served as a pretext and, wrote the author,

They [the soldiers] came back after a while and stormed the house, smashing the windows with stones. Truly a heroic storming of a fortress held by women! They destroyed everything in the house, and the women and children were obliged to flee to Mrs. Scheffers at Klein Kafferkraal, where I met them. We know of many cases of cruelty and violence, cases that have roused us to a passion of hatred.

A celebrated Boer general, Christiaan de Wet, wrote this scathing account about the treatment of women and children:

When the capturing of women, or rather the war against them and against the possessions of the Boer commenced, they took to bitter flight to remain at least out of the hands of the enemy... Many a smart, well-bred daughter rode on horseback and urged the cattle on, in order to keep out of the hands of the pursuers as long as at all possible, and not to be carried away to the concentration camps, which the British called Refugee Camps (Camps of Refuge). How incorrect, indeed! Could anyone ever have thought before the war that the twentieth century could show such barbarities? No.

De Wet concluded this account by terming it a shameful history.

21

Civil Religion, Afrikanerdom and the Republic

In this section, I will be brief, because with the end of the (Second) Anglo-Boer War, the formal history of the Boers of the Transvaal came to an end – by which I mean that it was the end of their existence as a separate political entity. Instead, at this point, the history of united Afrikanerdom made a stuttering start.

In 1902, the representatives of the two Boer republics surrendered almost unconditionally. Forty-six years later, during 1948, the National Party, which was supported almost entirely by Afrikaner votes, took power in the Union of South Africa. Once again, a government consisting only of Afrikaans-speakers held power – but now it governed all South Africa. Twelve years later, after a referendum that was carried by a small majority, the National Party government declared South Africa a republic. To many Afrikaners, the republic was the fulfilment of the aspirations of the two Boer republics, which had aimed not only to retain their independence under control of the *volk*, but to unify all South Africa under Boer-Afrikaner leadership.

In 1910, the two former Boer republics and the two former British colonies united to become the Union of South Africa, with Louis Botha, former commander of the Boer forces, as its first prime minister. Some of the significant features of the union were that Dutch and English were recognised as co-official languages and white supremacy was entrenched, with the vote being restricted to white people (except for the Cape Province, where the non-white Cape Qualified Franchise was retained until it was progressively reduced over time).

With the creation of the Union, all Dutch-speaking whites (who were already known as Afrikaners) were now members of the same polity. Increasingly, Dutch-speaking whites, whether formerly Boers of the two republics or Afrikaners of the two colonies, identified themselves as members of one, self-ascribed, Afrikaner *volk*.

Broadly, after union, Afrikaners went in two political directions. One direction, which was dominant until 1948, favoured cooperation and united political action by the two main white groups, namely the Afrikaans-speakers and English-speakers. The leading politicians in this stream were the two former Boer generals, Louis Botha and Jan Smuts, in the South African Party. The opposing stream, which campaigned against Anglicisation and more actively promoted Afrikaner rights and welfare, was led by another former Boer general, J.B.M. Hertzog, in the National Party. In time, Hertzog formed an alliance with Smuts in the United Party, and left the National Party to others, only to rejoin it later when it reconstituted itself as the Reunited National Party or HNP.

This brief overview does not do justice to the complexity and turbulence that characterised white South African politics during the period from the early 1900s to 1948. In addition, it does not at all mention the developments in non-white politics during that period. For instance, the African National Congress, which came to power in 1994 and so ended the era of dominant white politics, was founded in 1912, largely in reaction to the exclusion of black people from political and civil rights in the Union.

Along with the turbulence of formal politics, there was also turbulence as Afrikaners struggled to define their image and identity. In much that follows, I am leaning heavily on the writing of T. Dunbar Moodie, who covered the ground extensively in his book *The Rise of Afrikanerdom* (1975). Moodie identified the central aspect of this struggle as the development of an Afrikaner civil religion, about which he wrote,

Certainly by 1938, the ordinary Afrikaner had made the main

themes of the civil religion part of his own emotional identity. Most Afrikaners believed that they belonged to an elect People, most believed that at some time in the future, and sooner rather than later, God would give them another republic...

Moodie traced the genesis of this civil religion to a series of speeches that Paul Kruger gave at the Paardekraal monument during his terms as president of the ZAR. (Paardekraal was where the Boers confirmed their resistance to the British annexation of the Transvaal in 1877.) For instance, in his *Memoirs*, Kruger recalled that in his speech at the celebration at the monument in 1888, he set out his view of the history of his people in the light of God's word, and called on everyone to humble themselves and to acknowledge 'the wonders of God's dealings with the people of the Republic'. The last sentiment, namely 'the wonders of God's dealings...' was crucial to the development of the civil religion: it postulated not only that God had a special interest in the Boers, but that there was a divine purpose for their existence within their own political sphere, namely their independent republic. The theology was also infused with the reward and retribution teachings of the Old Testament prophets, namely that God rewarded good and faithful behaviour and punished errant behaviour, even to the destruction of the nation. And why should God care so much, and take such an interest, in such a small and separate people? Why was such a small and isolated group of people so capable of delighting or angering God? Because they were special, far more so than any other group with which they interacted – that was why.

Moodie explained that the independence of the republic became a key belief of Kruger's civil faith. Kruger also believed that, because the Boers had a special covenant with God, if they failed him, one of the ways in which they could be punished was to have their independence taken from them. However, in Moodie's view, the earlier version of the civil religion, from the early 1900s until the early 1930s, only reached back to the Second Anglo-Boer War. During this period, Afrikaners searched for meaning in the suffering and deprivation of the war period, and looked to make it the basis of countrywide Afrikaner unity and identity.

Moodie wrote that the election victory of 1948, which the National Party won with a small majority of five seats, 'owed no small thanks' to the civil religion, to Christian National ideology, and to the *Broederbond*'s practical assistance. The Afrikaner *Broederbond* (Afrikaner Brotherhood), which was founded in 1918, was a secret, exclusively male organisation that restricted its membership to Afrikaans-speakers who were also Calvinists. The *Broederbond* was dedicated to the advancement of Afrikaner interests; as it grew in size and influence, it infiltrated commanding sectors such as education, the civil service, business and commerce, and politics. Its influence can be seen, for instance, in the fact that every prime minister and state president of South Africa from 1948 to the end of apartheid in 1994 was a member of the *Broederbond*.

Christian Nationalism was the ideology that underlay both the civil religion and the elaborations of the apartheid policy that the National Party government called separate development. The main ideological strands of Christian Nationalism can be summarised as follows: it was based on the belief that God's highest creation in the human sphere is the nation (*volk*) and that man's highest spiritual calling is service to the nation; it conceived of the nation as a static and permanently enduring entity; it rejected notions of individual freedom and inviolable rights because the highest freedom is found in service to the nation (cf. Diederichs); it defined the *volk* as white and Afrikaner, with a higher calling to guardianship over non-whites (cf. Meyer) because they were less advanced in realising their divine identity and mission; and it viewed apartheid as the political means to allow various co-existing nations to realise their separate callings and identities.

The influence of Christian National ideologues such as Diederichs and Meyer can be seen from the fact that the former was chairman of the *Broederbond* (1938–1942), National Party member of parliament (1953–1975), Minister of Economic Affairs (1958–1967), Minister of Mines

(1961–1964), Minister of Finance (1967–1975), and State President (1975–1997), while Meyer was chairman of the *Broederbond* (1960–1972) and chairman of the board of the South African Broadcasting Corporation (1959–1980). Meyer propagated Christian National ideology and *Broederbond* aims by turning the SABC into a propaganda organ of the government, so that by 1977 there were at least forty-nine *Broeders* in the organisation, and by 1978 at least four members of the nine-member board of the SABC were *Broeders*. Meyer was appointed by Albert Hertzog, Minister of Post and Telecommunication, who had played a leading role in the development of the *Broederbond*. Under successive National Party governments, infiltrations and transformations of this kind took place wherever possible, in as many organisations and spheres as possible.

Moodie regarded the 1930s as the crucial period for the wider development of the civil religion. At this time, said Moodie, Afrikaner writers pushed back the sacred history from its origins in Boer War suffering to the epic of the Great Trek, and showed the close connection between them. The most formative of all events during this period was the celebration of the centenary of the Great Trek in 1938. From a small beginning, it became an event that galvanised and united many Afrikaners to identify with a history that revealed a divine purpose through the trek, through epic battles such as Blood River, through the covenant, through struggles for independence and nationhood against British imperialism and African enemies, through the denigration and suffering of the Anglo-Boer War, and finally through the awakening consciousness of the Afrikaner *volk*.

The centenary celebration began when wagons, named after key *Voortrekker* leaders and iconic trekker events and themes, travelled across the country from various starting points. The first wagon began its journey at the foot of the Jan van Riebeeck statue in Cape Town, to celebrate the arrival of Dutch/European settlers in Southern Africa, and the event ended in Pretoria with the laying of the foundation for the Voortrekker Monument. A huge crowd attended the event.

The Voortrekker Monument, Pretoria, constructed to commemorate the centenary of the Great Trek.

During the first part of the twentieth century, while Afrikaners were divided by politics, by questions of strategy, and even by the issue of the republic, there was growing enthusiasm and unity around the question of language. Moodie wrote that one of the most important wellheads of the Afrikaner civil faith was the fight for official recognition of Afrikaans and for its equality with English in everyday life. The struggle for Afrikaans became one of the most powerful factors that united Afrikaners in what was called *volkseenheid* (unity of the people). Afrikaans came to be regarded as a gift from God for unique self-expression, and as an essential marker of ethnicity that kept Afrikaners distinct and separate within the plan of a God-given particularity. Although Afrikaans replaced Dutch as one of the official languages in 1925, the *taalstryd* (language struggle) continued, and even intensified, against the dominance of English with its international status, widespread use, commercial support and much larger number of speakers (viewed globally).

The common thread that ran through white politics, no matter how complex and turbulent the political developments were, and no matter how many acrimonious divisions there were, was that all parties were united on the need to maintain white domination. As Moodie said, from the beginning of the eighteenth century, white racism was a constant factor in Afrikaner history – there was to be no equality between black and white in any area where the Afrikaner had his/her say. However, Moodie pointed out that English-speaking white South Africans were just as racist as Afrikaners.

When the National Party (strictly, the Reunited National Party or HNP) gained power in 1948, it was largely because of its race policy. Although the HNP's appeal to Afrikaner unity and interests was important, it was ancillary to the question of race. While the HNP pledged to implement a policy of strict racial segregation (or apartheid) in all spheres of life, Smuts's United Party was seen by many to be soft and vague on race. Opponents claimed that, far from preserving separation and domination, United Party policy would eventually lead to racial integration.

After its election victory, the National Party focused on racial policy and began to develop and implement separate development as a refinement and elaboration of apartheid. Essentially, separate development was an attempt to make apartheid more acceptable to a critical world by positing that, although white and black people would be strictly separate and sovereign in their own domains, they would nevertheless be equal. It was ideological subterfuge that fooled no one, neither the subjugated people nor supporters of the policy, as to its real intentions. On the other hand, after 1948 the Afrikaner civil religion began to fade into the background as a political theme and was only articulated when politicians felt a special need to rally support.

Although, for political reasons, the issue of the republic was not prominent during the 1948 election campaign, it was always prominent in the civil religion. Moodie explained the connection by saying that the future republic linked the past and the future, making an appeal to the Afrikaner past, a reminder of the coming glory. It was no surprise, therefore, that the issue of the republic re-emerged in white politics after the National Party consolidated its hold on power in the 1953 and 1958 elections. However, when the referendum on the republic was held during 1960, the issues were not so much Afrikaner eschatology as promoting the unity of the two white races in the face of growing world condemnation and spreading resistance to apartheid by black South Africans. The referendum was carried by a slim majority and the republic came into being on 31 May 1961. This was a deliberate gesture to history, as it was the same date on which the Anglo-Boer War officially ended in 1902, the date of the establishment of the Union of South Africa in 1910, and the date when the South African flag (next to the British Union Jack) was first flown in 1928.

I was born in South Africa in 1944; in 1948, the National Party was elected to government and introduced apartheid; and on 31 May 1961, in the city of Port Elizabeth, reluctantly, I marched as a school cadet at a function to mark the inauguration of the Republic of South Africa. In the long view of history, this Boer ideal of the Afrikaner-dominated republic did not last for long; Afrikaner and white political dominance ended only thirty-three years later when Nelson Mandela was inaugurated as president of South Africa on 10 May 1994.

During the first fifty years of my life, from 1944 to 1994, I lived, worked, married and raised my family in apartheid-ruled South Africa and Namibia, except for four years during which I lived in other countries. Although this book is about the Boers of the Transvaal, at another level it is about the times in which I grew up and which had such a profound influence on me: the times that were so deeply influenced by Afrikaner history, even though I am not an Afrikaner, and by the beliefs, experiences and fate of the Boers of the Transvaal.

Here at the end of this journey into the past, have I reached a greater level of understanding about the forces that shaped me, even as

I began more and more to interrogate them, and to push back against them? I have – but it can't be summed up in only a few sentences. However, I will set down a few thoughts. I have developed a much deeper understanding of the experiences that shaped the Boers' (and thus the Afrikaners') views of themselves and the world. I have a deeper appreciation of the causes, and features, of the peculiarly isolated and isolationist nature of their society. And I have understood more clearly how they came to develop their mythology. I have also come to understand more clearly why the Afrikaner version of segregation (apartheid), under which I grew up and lived, and which troubled me for so many years, was so uniquely rigid, so peculiarly isolationist and so intent on defining and maintaining borders and boundaries. (This is not to suggest that apartheid was any more, or less, harsh or forbidding than other forms of segregation. That discussion should be conducted elsewhere.) For the rest, I will reflect, and continue to reflect, on what I have read, constructed, written and learned.

Finally, I hope that the reader has enjoyed this exploration and has found it rewarding.

Notes

1. This was once a part of the colonial frontier near the Great Fish River in the Eastern Cape region of South Africa. It was well known for its fractious and rebellious Boer population.
2. This was also the locality in which Pringle and his party were settled in 1820.
3. Both terms are disputed and are claimed to be derogatory. However, no one has ever come up with satisfactory substitutes
4. This is a reference to Walter Scott's novel *A Legend of Montrose*, which features the MacEagh clan, who are also known as 'the Children of the Mist'. Incidentally, Scott, who was one of Pringle's patrons, used his influence with leading British politicians to support Pringle's application for him and his family party to be included among the settlers who were sent to the Eastern Cape Colony in 1820.
5. This might be east of Williston in the Karoo, about 500 kilometres north-east of Cape Town.
6. The sjambok is a long, tapered whip that was usually made of rhinoceros or hippopotamus hide; nowadays it is often made of hardened plastic.
7. The Bechuana people occupied the territory north of the Orange River in what was later called the Northern Cape, as well as in present-day Botswana (formerly Bechuanaland).
8. 'Oorlam' is said to be a Malay word meaning 'from the east'. In time, it acquired the connotation of 'learned' and 'skilful' and was applied to a number of mixed-race groups who lived beyond the colonial frontier but used European technology and methods.
9. In 1820, the number of colonists increased significantly when the 4,000 newly arrived British men, women and children were settled on the eastern frontier.
10. As an example, during the late 1920s, my father as a young man was a trainee officer in the British Merchant Navy. His contract allowed him full board and lodging, uniforms and instruction

towards passing exams. Of course, he provided his services as a seaman and, as he gained qualifications, as a junior officer. His remuneration was five pounds for three years. When I expressed surprise at how little he was paid, my father replied, 'My boy, we were lucky to get even that much.'

11. 'Nagmaal' translates literally as 'evening meal' but actually means 'holy communion'.
12. Conan Doyle estimated that, at this stage of the war, about 15,000 Boer fighters had been taken prisoner, while about 10,000 had given up the fight.

Works Cited

Adhikari, Mohamed. 2013. 'European livestock farmers and hunter-gatherer societies: a genocidal collision'. *Global Dialogue*, 15:1, Winter/Spring

Aylward, Alfred. 1881. *The Transvaal of to-day: war, witchcraft, sport, and spoils in South Africa*. Edinburgh and London: William Blackwood and Son

Backhouse, James. 1844. *A narrative of a visit to the Mauritius and South Africa*. York: Hamilton, Adams and Co.

Barrow, John. 1801. *An account of travels into the interior of Southern Africa in the years 1797 and 1798*. London (privately published)

Becker, Charles. 1878. *Guide to the Transvaal*. Dublin: J. Dollard

Borcherds, Petrus Bochardus. 1861. *An autobiographical memoir*. (reissue) Cape Town: African Connoisseurs Press

Bryce, James. 1899. *Impressions of South Africa* (3rd edition). London: Macmillan

Campbell, John. 1815. *Travels in South Africa*. London: Black and Parry

Cappon, James. 1901. *Britain's title in South Africa, or, The story of Cape Colony to the days of the great trek*. London, New York: Macmillan

Chesson, F.W. 1871. *The Dutch republics of South Africa*. London: William Tweedie

Cloete, Henry and William Brodrick Cloete, ed. 1899. *The history of the great Boer trek and the origin of the South African republics*. London: J. Murray

Creswicke, Louis. 1900. *South Africa and the Transvaal War, Volume One*. Edinburgh: T.C. and E.C. Jack and Manchester: Kenneth Maclennan

De Wet, Christiaan. 1902. *Three years war* (1st American edition). New York: Charles Scribner's Sons

Diederichs, N. 1936. *Nationalisme as lewensbeskouing*. Bloemfontein: Nasionale Pers

Doyle, Arthur Conan. 1900. *The Great Boer War*. London: Smith, Elder and Co.

Eybers, G.W. 1918. *Select constitutional documents illustrating South African history, 1795–1910.* London: George Routledge and Sons

Eyre, John. 1845. *Journals of expeditions of discovery into central Australia and overland from Adelaide to King George's Sound in the years 1840–1: Volume 1.* London: T. and W. Boone

Fitzpatrick. James Percy. 1899. *The Transvaal from within: a private record of public affairs.* London: William Heinemann

Fisher, William Edward Garrett. 1896. *The Transvaal and the Boers: a short history of the South African Republic, with a chapter on the Orange Free State.* New York: Negro Universities Press

Harrison, David. 1981. *The white tribe of Africa.* Berkeley and Los Angeles: University of California Press

Heckford, Sarah. 1882. *A lady trader in the Transvaal.* London: S. Low, Marston, Searle and Rivington

Latrobe, Christian. 1818. *Journal of a visit to South Africa in 1815 and 1816: with some account of the missionary settlements of the United Brethren, near the Cape of Good Hope.* New York, J. Eastburn and Co.

Lichtenstein, Hinrich. 1815. *Travels in Southern Africa in the years 1803, 1804, 1805 and 1806* (translated by Anne Plumtree), London: Henry Colburn

Marcosson, Isaac Frederick. 1921. *An African adventure.* New York: John lane Co.

Massie, R.H. 1905. *The native tribes of the Transvaal.* Great Britain: War Office

Meyer, P. 1941. 'Grondslae van die Afrikaanse republikeinse staatsvorming', in J. Coetzee, P. Meyer and N. Diederichs, 1941. *Ons republiek.* Bloemfontein: Nasionale Pers

Moodie, J. W. D. 1835. *Ten years in South Africa.* London: Richard Bentley

Moodie, T. Dunbar. 1975. *The rise of Afrikanerdom: power, apartheid, and the Afrikaner civil religion.* Berkeley, Los Angeles and London: University of California Press

Philip, John. 1828. *Researches in South Africa.* London: James Duncan

Pringle, Thomas. 1834. *Narrative of a residence in South Africa.* Brentwood: Doppler Press

Reid, Mayne. 1907. *The Vee-Boers.* London: George Routledge and Sons

Reitz, F.W. 1900, *A century of wrong.* London: 'Review of Reviews' Office

Stanley, H.M. 1898. *Through South Africa.* London: Sampson, Low, Marston and Company

Theal, George McCall. 1886.

History of the emigrant Boers in South Africa; or The wanderings and wars of the emigrant farmers from their leaving the Cape Colony to the acknowledgment of their independence by Great Britain. London: Swan, Sonnenschein, Lowry and Co.

Thompson, George. 1827. *Travels and adventures in Southern Africa*. London: Henry Colburn

Turner, Frederick Jackson. 1921. *The frontier in American history*. New York: Henry Holt and Company

Twain, Mark. 1897. *Following the equator: a journey around the world*. Hartford: American Publishing Co.

Uitlander. 1917. *Een en ander over het dorpsleven in Transvaal*. No publisher stated

Van Warmelo, Dietlof. 1902. *On commando*. London: Methuen

www.ingramcontent.com/pod-product-compliance
Lightning Source LLC
Chambersburg PA
CBHW071828080526
44589CB00012B/952